Pocket Charts for Emergent Readers

By Valerie SchifferDanoff

Consultant for ESL, Diane Maldonado

SCHOLASTIC PROFESSIONAL BOOKS

NEW YORK • TORONTO • LONDON • AUCKLAND • SYDNEY

Dedicated to the ones I love.

I'd like to acknowledge my husband. I guess you were right—

I did write more than one book.

Cover design by Vincent Ceci and Jaime Lucero
Cover photographs by Donnelly Marks
Interior photographs by Valerie SchifferDanoff
Interior design and illustrations by Solutions by Design, Inc.

ISBN 0-590-31470-X

Table of Contents

* *Especially good for ESL students.*

Introduction

The idea for this book grew out of the first pocket chart book, *The Pocket Chart Book.* For young and emergent readers who just love to touch everything, a versatile pocket chart in your classroom is invaluable. Using charts encourages a multisensory approach to language acquisition. A pocket chart is just the right size for these students, too, because it's *their* size. They'll take ownership of their learning as they walk right up to the chart to touch the words they are acquiring. Watch the colors of learning come alive as you brighten a space with a pocket chart!

Pocket charts work for all curriculum areas. They're a natural for all kinds of language arts activities. Written language looks great displayed on different color sentence strips set against different background colors provided by the pocket charts. For teaching dramatic play, you can write dialogue and narration on sentence strips in two different colors. The colors can also teach about quotation marks. For poetry, you can write verses in alternating colors or write rhyming words in matching colors. This is especially important for focusing on phonics. For art activities, you can write directions on sentence strips and store pieces and templates in the charts. For math, pocket charts provide a manipulative hands-on format. A pocket chart for special days can become a classroom tradition as children anticipate seeing it again and again or having it filled with something new.

Oh Where, Oh Where Can My Pocket Chart Go?

Pocket charts can be used anywhere in the classroom where you would like a poem, a center, an independent learning activity or a follow-up to a large group shared reading or small group guided reading experience.

How Can I Hang My Pocket Chart?

Pocket charts can be displayed on a bulletin board, secured by long heavy-duty push pins, or they can be hung from an easel with easel clips. Heavy-duty self-adhesive Velcro can also be used to hang pocket charts on walls or from shelves. Pocket chart stands are available at teaching supply stores.

You may find that pocket charts tend to roll inward when suspended. Placing a thin dowel cut to the width of the chart in the last pocket, behind the sentence strip can alleviate this problem. Dowels can be purchased at hardware or home stores or craft shops and cut to size.

When hanging pocket charts for young learners be especially aware of the height. The wonderful thing about pocket charts is that they can be hung at just the right height for children to use. Children love to be able to walk right up to the chart and easily reach into a pocket.

What Sizes of Pocket Charts and Sentence Strips Are Available?

Pocket charts are available in a variety of sizes and colors as are sentence strips. If you cannot afford more than one pocket chart, one is a good place to begin. The most versatile size is 42" x 58". However, purchasing more than one will prove to be one of the best investments you'll make for your language immersion program.

Other sizes available are 24" x 24" and 34" x 42". (The most common size for pocket charts is 34" x 42".)

POCKET CHART SUPPLY SOURCES

Teaching Resource Center Catalog (1-800-833-3389)

- The best source for purchasing pocket charts and sentence strips. Red, pink lavender, blue, yellow, green, and white pocket charts in various sizes are available in the catalog.

American Academic Supplies (1-800-325-9118)

- permanent markers, push pins, easel clips
- pocket charts (limited sizes, blue only), sentence strips, glitter writers, stickers, borders, tagboard, pregummed shapes, craft glue, Tru-Ray construction paper, multicultural construction paper, small manipulatives

Beckley-Cardy (1-800-227-1178)

- Pacon brand sentence strips (some of the best colors available)

Staples and Office Max stores

- good sources for Papermate bullet point markers which work very well on sentence strips

Other supplies are also available from the following catalogs:

J.L. Hammet Co. (1-800-333-4600)

The Reprint Corp. (1-800-248-9171)

Kaplan (1-800-334-2014)

Lakeshore (1-800-421-5354)

How Can I Store My Sentence Strips?

I like to organize my sentence strips by theme. I keep them in a flat folder or wrapped around the inside edge of the storage box in which I store all my theme materials. This prevents the sentence strips from getting rolled too tightly. A butterfly clip, large paper clip, or small binder clip will keep each set of sentence strips and the pocket chart pieces together.

While teaching a staff development course on pocket charts the teachers with whom I was working suggested these other storage ideas:

- a long stem flower box (ask a florist for one)
- a wall paper glue holder
- a box in which wall paper comes, cut along top
- the box in which the sentence strips arrived, covered with contact paper.

There are also commercial boxes available (see the section on supplies on page 6.)

Basic Teaching Techniques When Teaching from a Pocket Chart

You can apply many of the basic techniques that follow to all the pocket charts in this book.

- Model how to use the components in the pocket chart.
- Teach children how to place words, sentence strips, and templates in the pocket chart and how to carefully remove them.
- When brainstorming to create a pocket chart, encourage everyone to participate.
- Write words on sentence strips and cut them apart if necessary. As an alternative, have children cut the words apart and then place them in the pocket chart.
- When reading from a pocket chart, read chorally with children. Point to every word as you read.
- When teaching a short poem, chanting or repeating the verses or rhymes is enjoyable. Then encourage children to chant or repeat the poem to the natural rhythm that occurs. Children like to chant sets of rhyming words too.
- When teaching a poem or reading, write two sets of the words. Cut one set apart for children to match words or sequence. As an independent or group activity allow the children to repeat building the story.
- Use pictures in addition to or instead of words. This allows children to match words to pictures and pictures to words. Patterns for templates are provided for this type of activity and stickers are also suggested.
- For math activities use cutouts or stickers as manipulatives. They can be matched to the words.

Additional techniques, hints, and reminders are presented with each pocket chart developed in the chapters that follow. By pairing these basic teaching techniques with the examples in each chapter, you can extend and develop more ideas for teaching with pocket charts.

Why Use Pocket Charts for ESL?

Pocket charts are a great resource for English as a Second Language learners because students learn the second language in a meaningful and fun way. Activities are set up to allow for a comfortable environment where students are willing to take risks. Pocket charts easily lend themselves to the basic ESL teaching technique, Total Physical Response Approach (see below). When using pocket charts with ESL students, consider their oral language ability, ways they may demonstrate understanding, and thinking skills used.

Students with little or no experience in English are best helped to understand English through visuals, body language, and gestures. These students often show understanding nonverbally. They may point, touch, draw, gesture, or demonstrate an action in some way.

As students progress they begin to express themselves in English and respond to questions with single words or short phrases. Encourage students to pantomime situations such as: touch your toes, jump over the puddle, turn around.

As students' fluency increases, they will begin to respond to questions and conduct conversations using simple phrases and sentences. Extend these by role playing and dramatizing stories.

The pocket charts that have an ESL variation or designation are appropriate for students who are progressing through the above stages of oral language ability.

Basic Teaching Techniques for ESL Students

- Speak clearly and use longer pauses.
- Introduce vocabulary items by giving directions. For example:

  Pick up the green leaf.

  First pick up the leaf, then pick up the rake.
- Ask different level questions that have:

  yes/no responses

  either/or phrasing

  the words *who, what, where, why,* and *when* at the beginning
- Increase difficulty by combining actions such as: point and bring.
- Combine pantomime and short verbal and written responses.
- Total Physical Response Approach (TPR) was developed by James Asher in 1977. This technique works well with young ESL students at all stages of language development. It is based on the premise that student learning is more efficient and student involvement more active when students respond with appropriate actions to oral commands. A sequence for using pocket charts that encourages a TPR is:

  1. Setup all materials necessary to perform a routine.
  2. Teacher models action sequence while students look and listen.
  3. Students respond physically to the teacher's commands.

     * Repeat steps 2 and 3 as often as necessary on different occasions for students to internalize language.
  4. As language acquisition increases, students can make a written copy from pocket chart words and use this written copy to read commands aloud to each other. This will help increase sight word vocabulary and can be used as the subject of several mini-lessons.
  5. Students take turns leading the group or working in pairs commanding and responding physically in English. Students repeat a series of commands.

RESOURCES FOR POEMS

When choosing poems for emergent readers look for poems with simple language and uncomplicated text. Avoid too much symbolism. Short rhyming poems are best.

The Scholastic Integrated Language Arts Resource Book by Valerie SchifferDanoff (Scholastic Professional Books, 1995)

Building Literacy with Interactive Charts by Kristin Schlosser and Vicki L. Phillips (Scholastic Professional Books, 1992)

Animals Poems From A to Z by Meish Goldish (Scholastic Professional Books, 1995)

Thematic Poems, Songs, and Fingerplays by Meish Goldish (Scholastic Professional Books, 1994)

Read A-Loud Rhymes for the Very Young selected by Jack Prelutsky (Alfred A. Knopf, 1986)

Poems Just for Us! by Bobbi Katz (Scholastic Professional Books, 1995)

Poems You Can Count On by Sandra Liatsos (Scholastic Professional Books, 1995)

Sing a Song of Popcorn selected by Beatrice Schenk DeRegniers (Scholastic, 1988)

Blackberry Ink by Eve Merriam (William Morrow, 1985)

Hailstones and Halibut Bones by Mary O'Neill (Bantam, 1961)

Hand Rhymes collected by Marc Brown (Penguin, 1985)

Play Rhymes collected by Marc Brown (Penguin, 1987)

The Random House Book of Poetry selected by Jack Prelutsky (Random House, 1983)

Poetry Place Anthology (Scholastic, 1983)

You Be Good & I'll Be Night by Eve Merriam (William Morrow & Co. 1988)

Questions Poems of Wonder selected by Lee Bennet Hopkins (Harper Trophy, 1992)

What Can it Be? by Jacqueline A. Ball (Simon & Schuster, 1989)

June Is a Tune by Sarah Wilson (Simon & Schuster, 1994)

Pocket Charts for Phonics

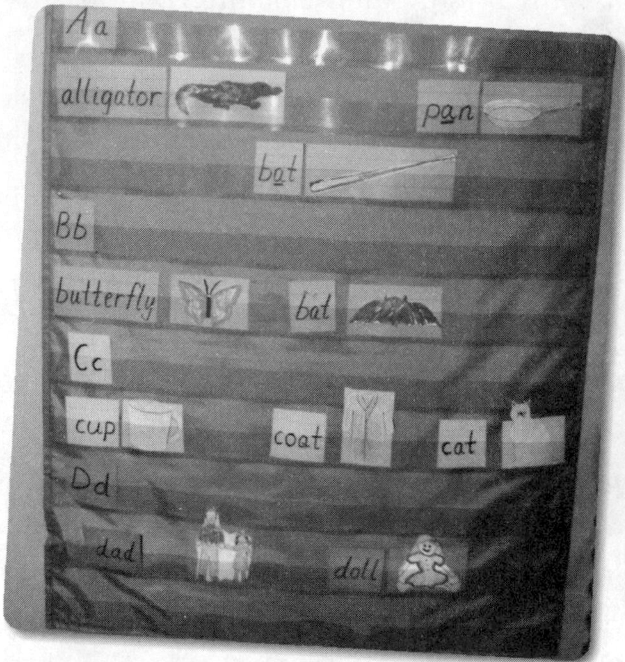

An understanding of sound/symbol relationships and the ability to break words down into their sounds are important skills for emergent readers. Students need to understand that words have beginning, middle, and ending sounds. A foundation in phonics contributes to success in reading.

A-Z Letter to Picture Match

PURPOSE

To identify letters of the alphabet and their corresponding sounds.

MATERIALS

- 42" x 58" pocket chart (or 24" x 24" or 34" x 34", depending on how much of the alphabet you want to do at a time)
- 12 sentence strips, 6 each in 2 different colors
- copies of a-z pictures (see box on page 11 and pages 17–28)
- scissors
- glue
- permanent marker
- colored pencils

The words chosen for the alphabet chart are words that begin with each letter and words in which the sound can be heard in the middle and at the end.

When teaching sound/symbol relationships, it is important to remember that the pronunciation of words can vary in regions of U.S., and that writing does not represent the spoken language perfectly. Presenting children with a variety of words that have the sound you are teaching at the beginning, end, and in the middle is helpful.

Additionally, some of the words can be used for more than one letter as is the case with pan, bat, bee, jet, etc. Encourage students to see how words might work for more than one sound.

An important consideration when teaching English as a Second Language students is that students may not have all the sounds in their native languages that are in English.

POCKET CHART LETTERS AND WORDS

A, a	alligator, pan, bat (baseball), ant
B, b	butterfly, bubble, bat (animal), bug
C, c	cup, cat, coat, cookie, circle
D, d	dad, doll
E, e	egg, three, bee, key, jet, wet
F, f	friend, flag, five
G, g	girl, gift
H, h	hat, hand
I, i	ice cream, kite, fish, inchworm, smile
J, j	juice, jack-in-the-box, jam jar
K, k	kitten, kite, kangaroo, key
L, l	leaf, ladybug, lollipop
M, m	mitten, mom
N, n	nut, nose, nest
O, o	go, over, boat, octopus, ocean, cone
P, p	pear, apple, peach pie
QU,qu	quilt, queen
R, r,	rainbow, river, rocket
S, s	scissors, soap, seal
T, t	teapot, two, ten
U, u	umbrella, sun, bus
V, v	van, valentine
W, w	watch, whale
X, x	box, fox, x marks the spot
Y, y	yo-yo, cherry yogurt
Z, z	zipper, zero, zebra

SETUP

1 Cut each of the sentence strips into 4"-pieces.

2 On each 4"-piece, write each letter in both upper and lower case. Alternate sentence strip colors for each letter pair for visual discrimination.

3 Color, cut, and glue each of the pictures onto sentence strips that are the same color of the sentence strips used for the letter on which you are focusing. (For example, if B, b is on a blue sentence strip, use a blue sentence strip piece for butterfly and bat.) Use the same color sentence strip to create a separate name card for each picture.

4 Place the letter cards in chart. Play a letter match game by holding up a picture then asking students to match it to the correct letter. Place the picture card and its matching name card in the correct letter pocket. Do the reverse, too: Place pictures and names in chart and hold up a letter. Have students respond chorally as you go through letters, pictures, and words. (For older students, you may want to just hold up name cards.)

5 Say the sound of the letter and play a picture/letter match game as above.

Variations

1 Place the letter cards in the chart. Have children draw pictures or cut out pictures from magazines of things whose names begin with different letters of the alphabet. Have them place each picture in the correct pocket in chart.

2 Play a letter-sort game by first letter or sound using 5-6 letters at a time.

Choose the letters you want to focus on, and place the letter cards in the box. Choose pictures that match each of the sounds. Have children take turns sorting the pictures into groups depending on which letter/sound each begins with. Have them place the pictures in the correct pocket on the chart.

3 Write each child's name on a sentence strip. Have him or her draw a small self-portrait or glue a small photo next to his or her name. Then have children place their name cards in the correct pocket of the chart corresponding to the letters/pictures.

4 Hand out letter and picture cards. Have students find their "matching student," and then have each of the pairs place the cards in the chart.

5 To focus on ending sounds, find or draw pictures of objects whose names end in each letter. Create label cards, and write the end letter (or letters) in a different color.

6 Set up the chart for independent practice by placing the letters in the chart, and the picture cards nearby, or vice versa.

Literature Integrations

There are a lot of great alphabet books. Having plenty available is very helpful. By asking students to bring one in, you're sure to get a variety. Here are some favorites.

Chicka Chicka Boom Boom by John Archambault and Bill Martin Jr. Simon & Schuster, 1989.

A is for Africa by Ifeoma Onyefulu. Dutton Books, 1993.

Eating the Alphabet by Lois Ehlert. Harcourt Brace Jovanovich, 1993.

Vowel Sounds

PURPOSE

To discriminate medial vowel sounds.

MATERIALS

- 24" x 24" or 34" x 42" pocket chart
- 25 white sentence strips (cut to size)
- 10 4"-pieces of sentence strips; 2 each in 5 different colors
- copies of vowel pictures (see pages 16–28)
- scissors
- marker
- glue
- colored pencils

POCKET CHART WORDS

(Make two copies of each vowel card.)

For a: pan, bat, hat, van, cat, dad, cake, rainbow, grapes, plane

For e: jet, wet, ten, nest, dress, shell, tree, bee, queen

For i: fish, gift, zipper, mitten, scissors, smile, kite, bride, child

For o: mom, teapot, doll, lollipop, stop (sign) go, yo-yo, boat, nose, zero

For u: bubble, bus, cup, sun, butterfly,

SETUP

1 Use two 4"-sentence strips in the same color to create two cards for each vowel. To help students focus on long and short vowels, on one card write the vowel itself in red, and on the other write the vowel in green.

2 Write the words on white sentence strip pieces. Write the long vowels in green and the rest of the word in black; write the short vowels in red and the rest of the word in black.

3 Color, cut, and glue pictures to sentence strips.

4 Work on one vowel at a time using long and short sounds. Hold up each word card, say the word, and then have children place words and pictures in chart.

5 Ask children to sort the words in the chart according to whether they have a long or short vowel sound. Say the words, chorally, stressing the vowel sound, several times to help students make this distinction.

6 Continue by comparing the two vowel sounds and having children sort the pictures under the correct vowel card in chart as you say the words.

7 As the children become more proficient at discriminating between long and short vowels, add more vowel sounds and generate some of your own words to add to the sorting activity.

Variations

1 When reading a book during reading group refer to and add to the chart with words from the story.

2 Write children's names on sentence strips and sort according to the vowel sound they contain.

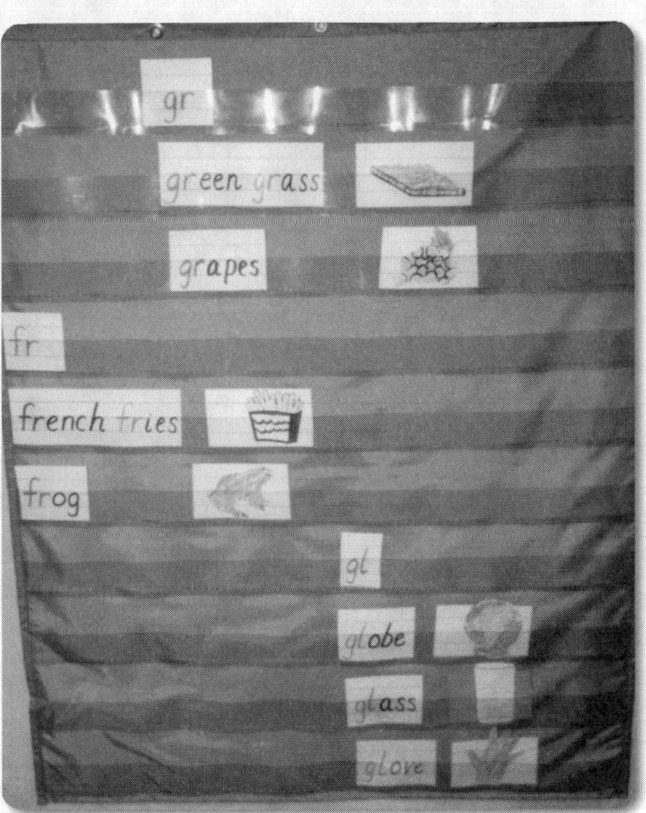

Consonant Blends and Digraphs

PURPOSE

To familiarize students with the letter combinations that form blends and digraphs. It is important that children be able to discriminate the two sounds that make up a blend. However, digraphs like *sh* cannot be heard as two separate sounds.

I've chosen to focus on the most commonly used and mispronounced consonant blends and digraphs. For instance, dr *as in dress and* tr *as in train are frequently confused with* ch *and* sh *especially when followed by r-controlled vowels.*

MATERIALS

- 34" x 42" pocket chart
- 32-40 sentence strips
- copies of pictures (pages 29–33)
- glue
- scissors

- colored pencils
- permanent markers

POCKET CHART WORDS

ch	child, chocolate chips, hatch
sh	shoe, shell, sheep, fish, shapes
th	think, tooth
gl	glove, glass, globe
cl	clap, clam
sn	snap, snow(flakes), snake
dr	dress, dragon, drum
br	bride, bread, brush
fr	frog, french fries
cr	cry, cracker, crane, crocodile
gr	grapes, green grass
tr	train, train tracks, trumpet
bl	blackbird, bluebird
fl	flower, flag, fly
pl	plane, plant
st	star, stop sign, store

SETUP

1. Write the blends and digraphs, as well as the words on separate sentence strip pieces. When writing the words use a different color marker for blends or digraphs. For example, for the word child, write *ch* in blue, and the rest of the word in black.

2. Color, cut, and glue pictures to sentence strip pieces.

3. Introduce one blend or digraph at a time. Place these in chart. Hold up a picture. Have the children say its name, then place the card in the chart.

4. After you've introduced two blends or digraphs, review them by placing the cards for each in the chart. Have children sort pictures and or words by sound. Increase the difficulty by adding more sounds in the pocket chart.

5. After all the blends and digraphs have been introduced, set up the chart for independent practice.

To help students understand how digraphs work, explain to them that sometimes two letters together form a new sound. (I like this saying too, s and h got married and now they're sh (say the new sound).)

Rhyme Sort

PURPOSE

To discriminate words that rhyme and categorize rhyming words.

MATERIALS

- 34" x 42" pocket chart
- sentence strips

- copies of pictures (pages 34–37)
- marker
- glue
- scissors

POCKET CHART WORDS

You can rhyme a row. Where does each word go?

Words in the Woods

snake, cake, lake, bake, rake, fake, make, wake

bat, cat, hat, fat, mat, sat, pat, rat

log, hog, frog, fog, dog

tree, bee, see, knee, flea, he, she, me

Sky Words

sun, fun, bun, ton, done, won, none, run

sky, try, fry, my, high, by, cry, pie, tie, why

star, car, far, jar, bar, tar

moon, tune, spoon, loon, baboon, dune, cartoon, noon, soon

First word is the key word.

SETUP FOR RHYMING

Use pictures alone, words alone, or pictures and words together depending on the ability of your students.

1. Write each set of words on sentence strips. Cut to size.
2. Copy, color, cut, and glue pictures to sentence strips.
3. For each category say key words with class and place in chart. Show and say rhyming words randomly and have children place them correctly in chart in a row.

Be sure to tell the children that rhyming words are not necessarily spelled the same, but sound the same.

SETUP FOR CATEGORIZING

1. Write each set of key words and category words on sentence strips. Cut to size.
2. Place categories in chart.
3. Say and show key words. Have children sort by category.

OTHER POSSIBLE RHYMES AND CATEGORIES

Playground Words

ball, tall, fall, hall, call, mall, stall, wall

run, fun, bun, ton, none, sun, won

ground, pound, round, around, found

play, day, may, way, hay, jay, lay, pay

swing, thing, ring, sing, wing, king, ding

Beach Words

sand, hand, and, land, band

shore, more, core, door, four, for, store

fish, dish, wish

swim, him, limb, dim, gym, rim

beach, teach, reach, peach

wet, set, get, jet, met, net, bet, let, pet

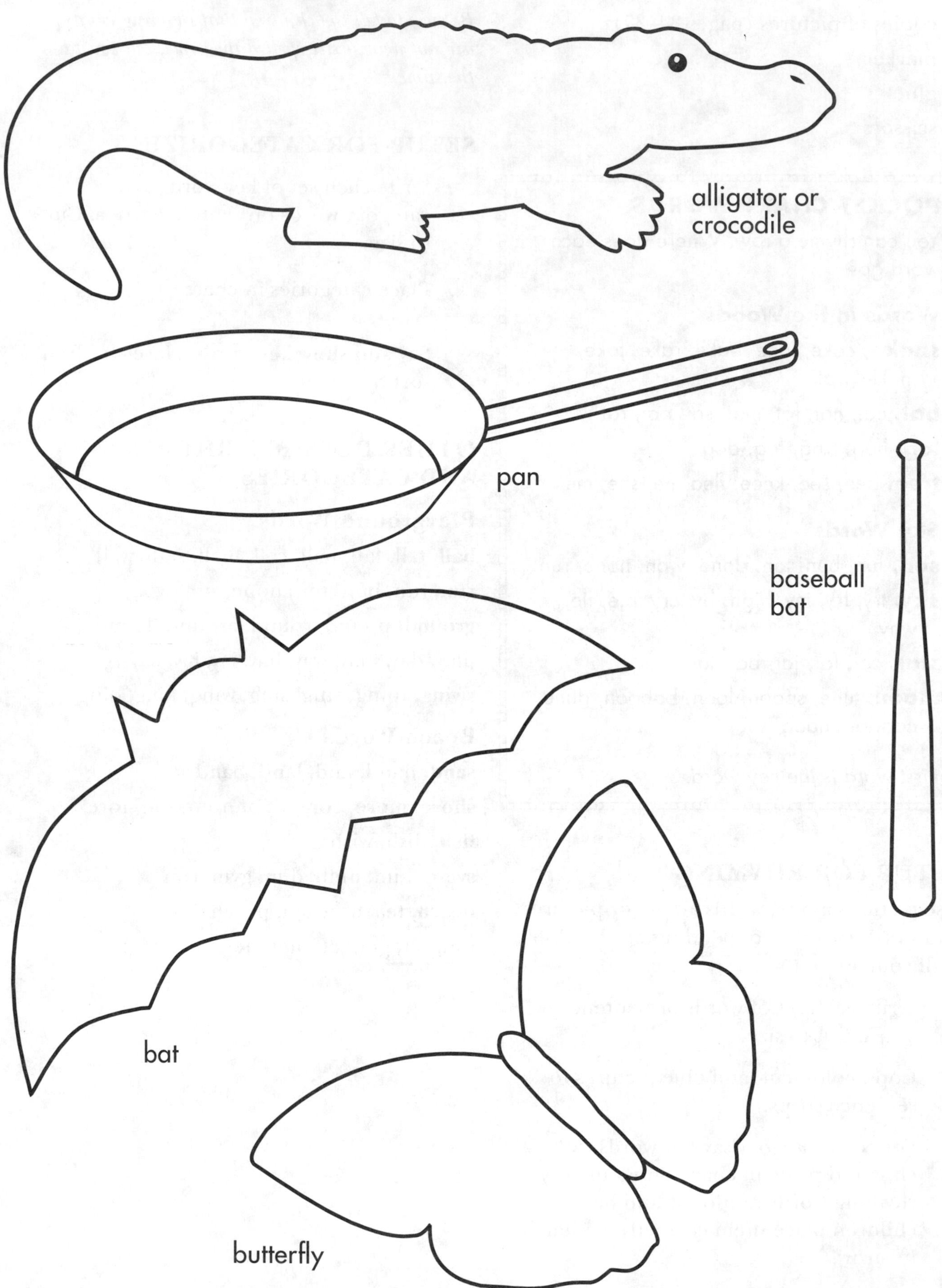
alligator or
crocodile
pan
baseball
bat
bat
butterfly

A–Z Letter to Picture Match and Vowel Sounds

doll
egg
jet or plane
three
fork

flag
five
girl
gift
hat

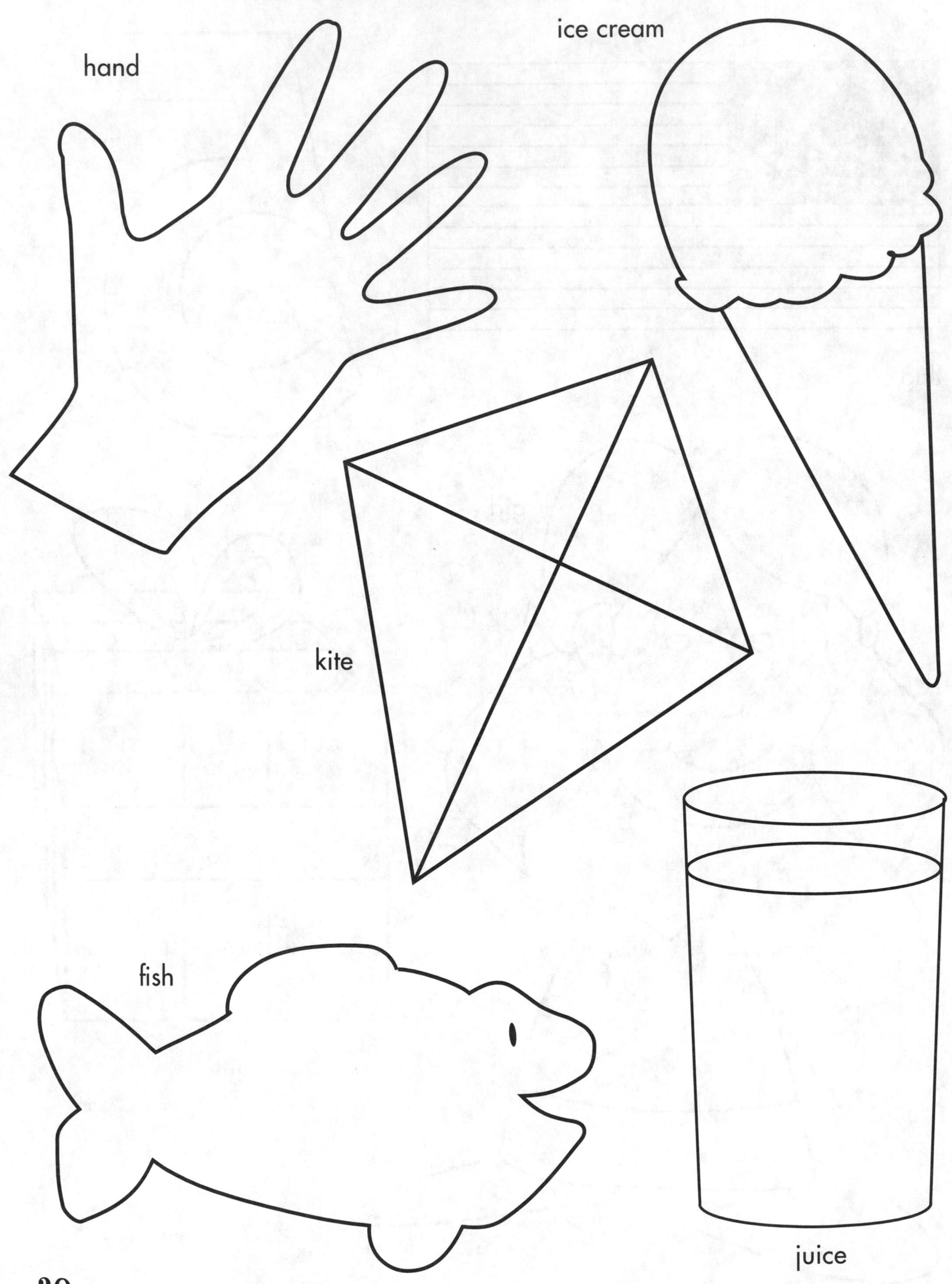
hand
ice cream
kite
fish
juice

jack-in-the-box
jam jar
leaf
kangaroo
kitten

A–Z Letter to Picture Match and Vowel Sounds

For nut see page 85.

A–Z Letter to Picture Match and Vowel Sounds

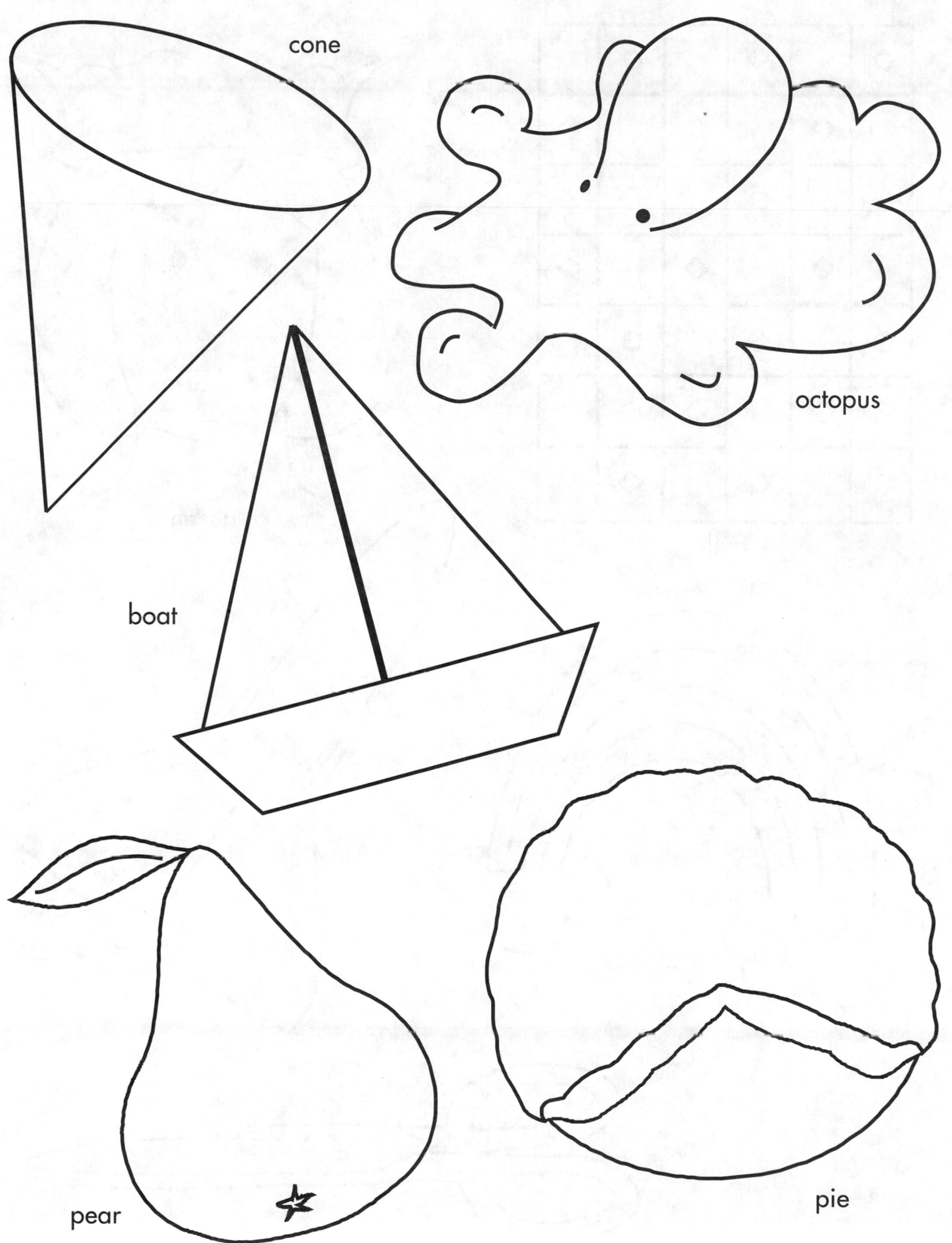

A–Z Letter to Picture Match and Vowel Sounds

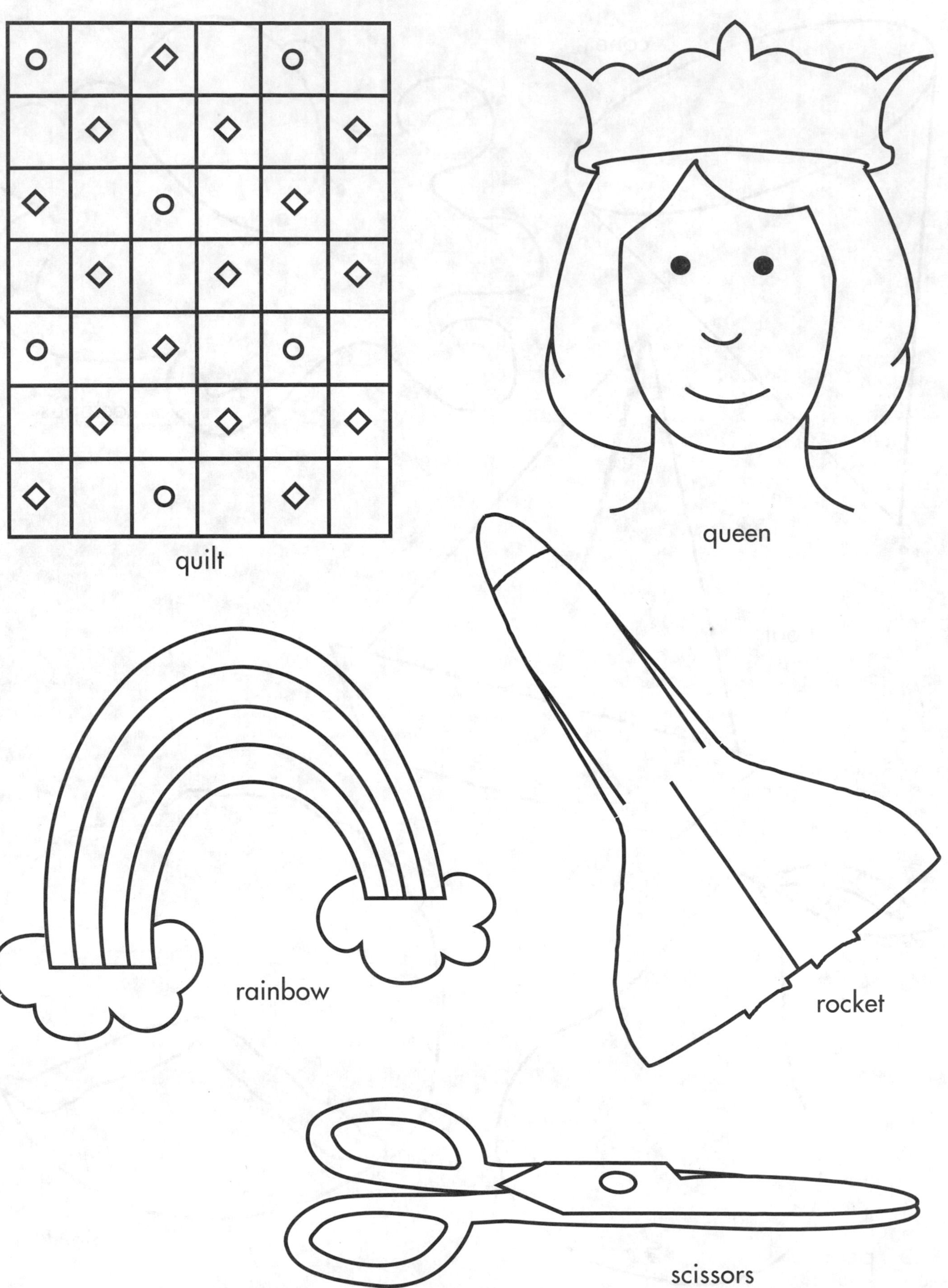

SOAP
seal
soap
teapot
two
ten

A–Z Letter to Picture Match and Vowel Sounds

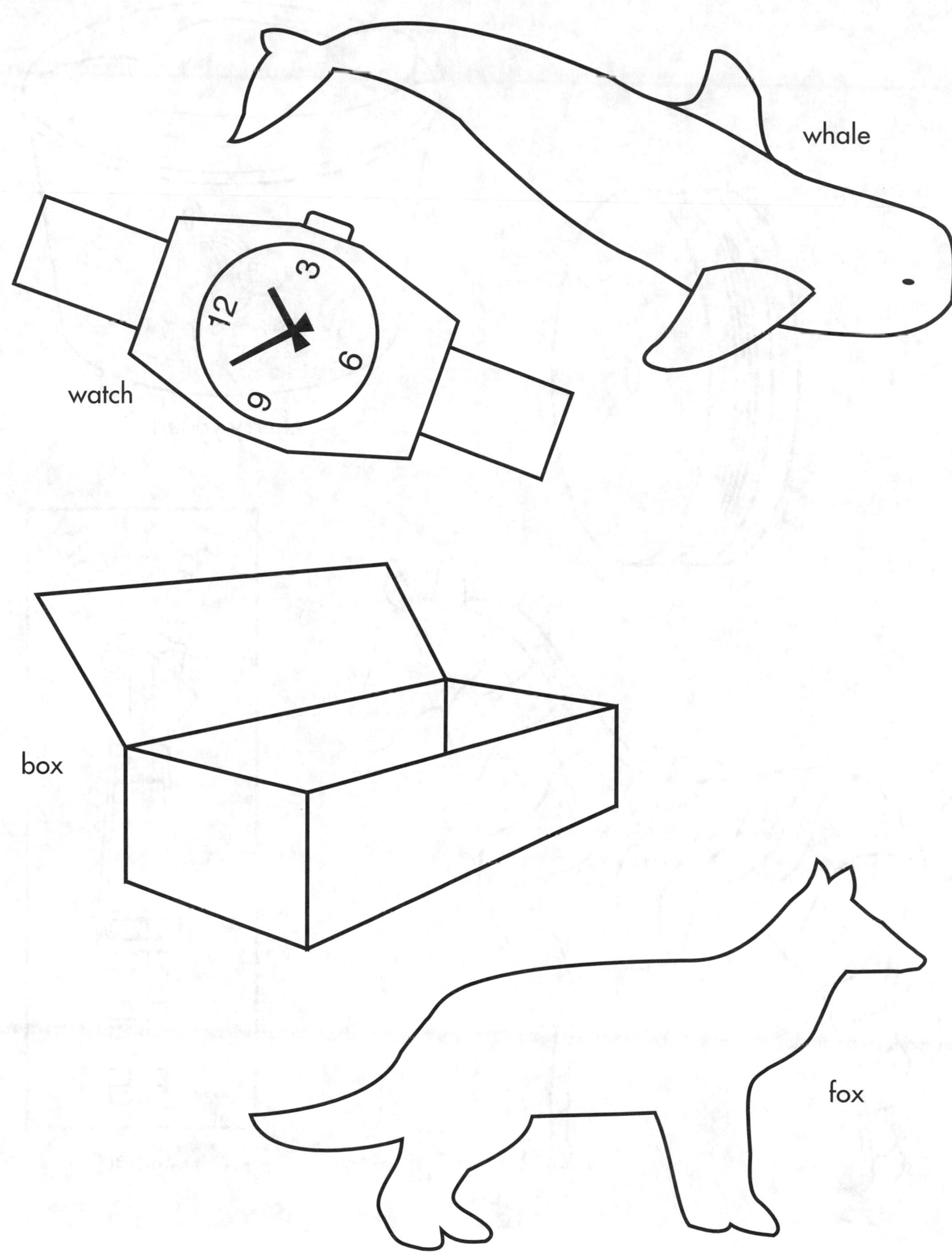
whale
3
12
6
9
watch
box
fox

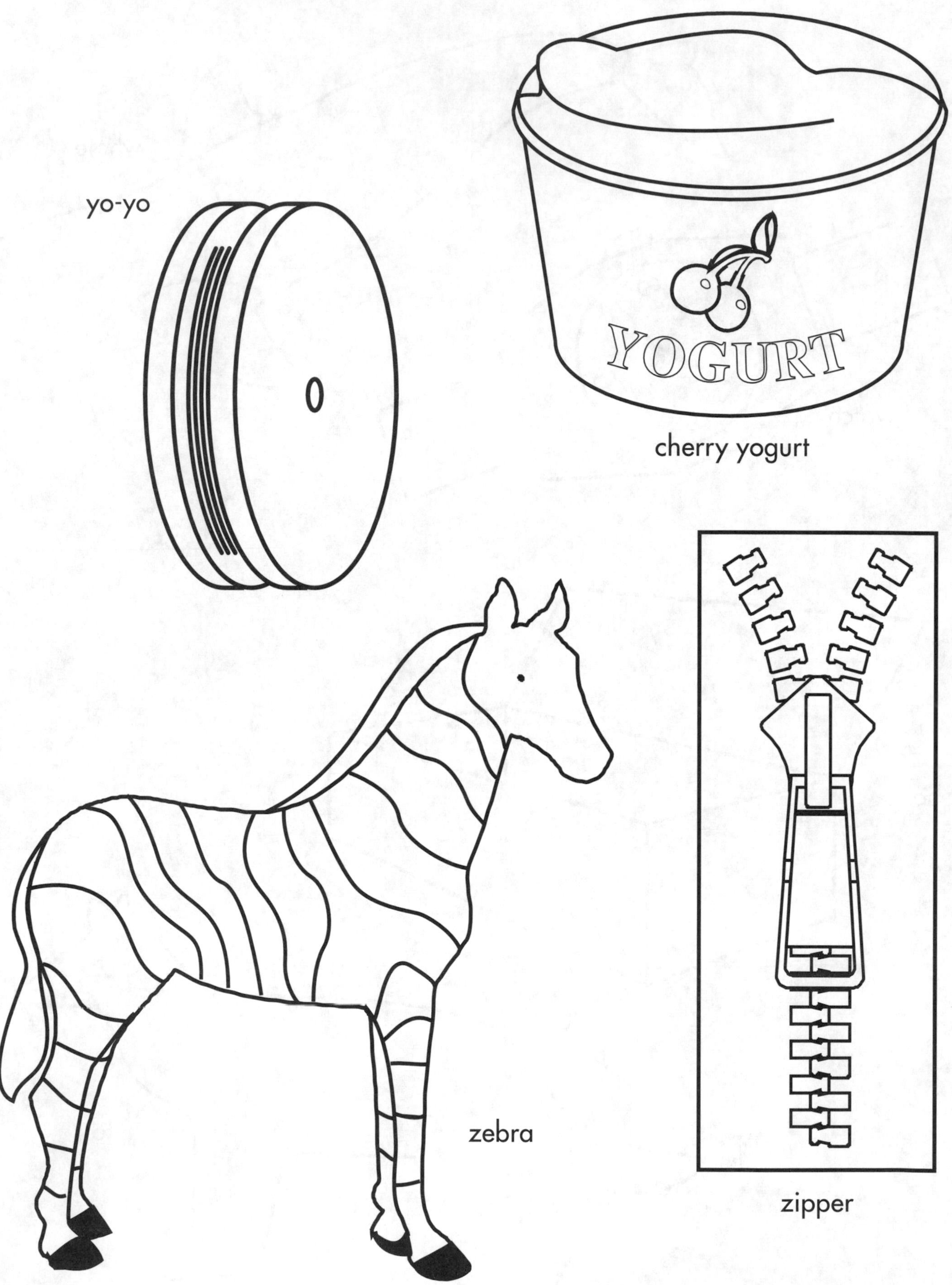
yo-yo
YOGURT
cherry yogurt
zebra
zipper

Consonant Blends and Digraphs

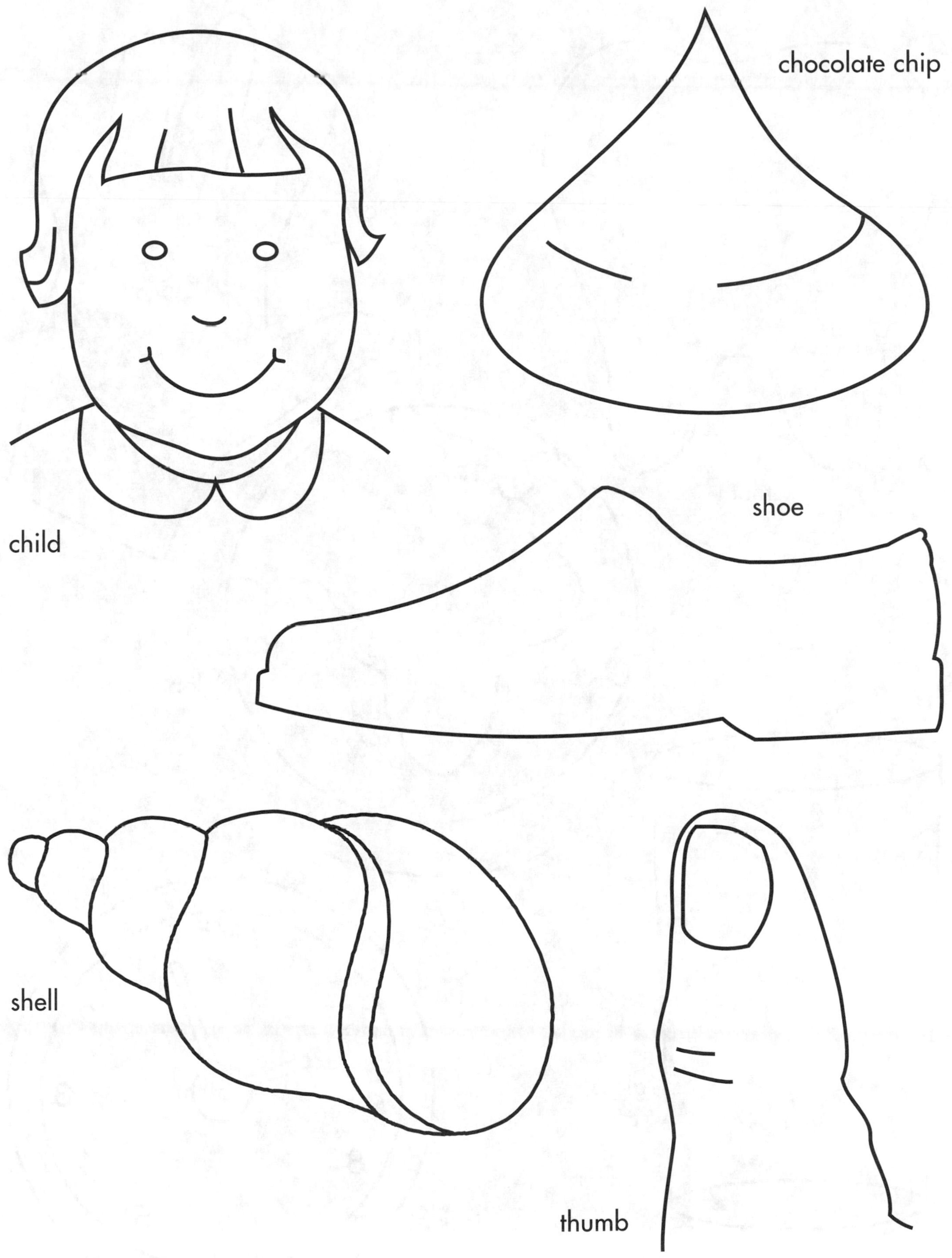

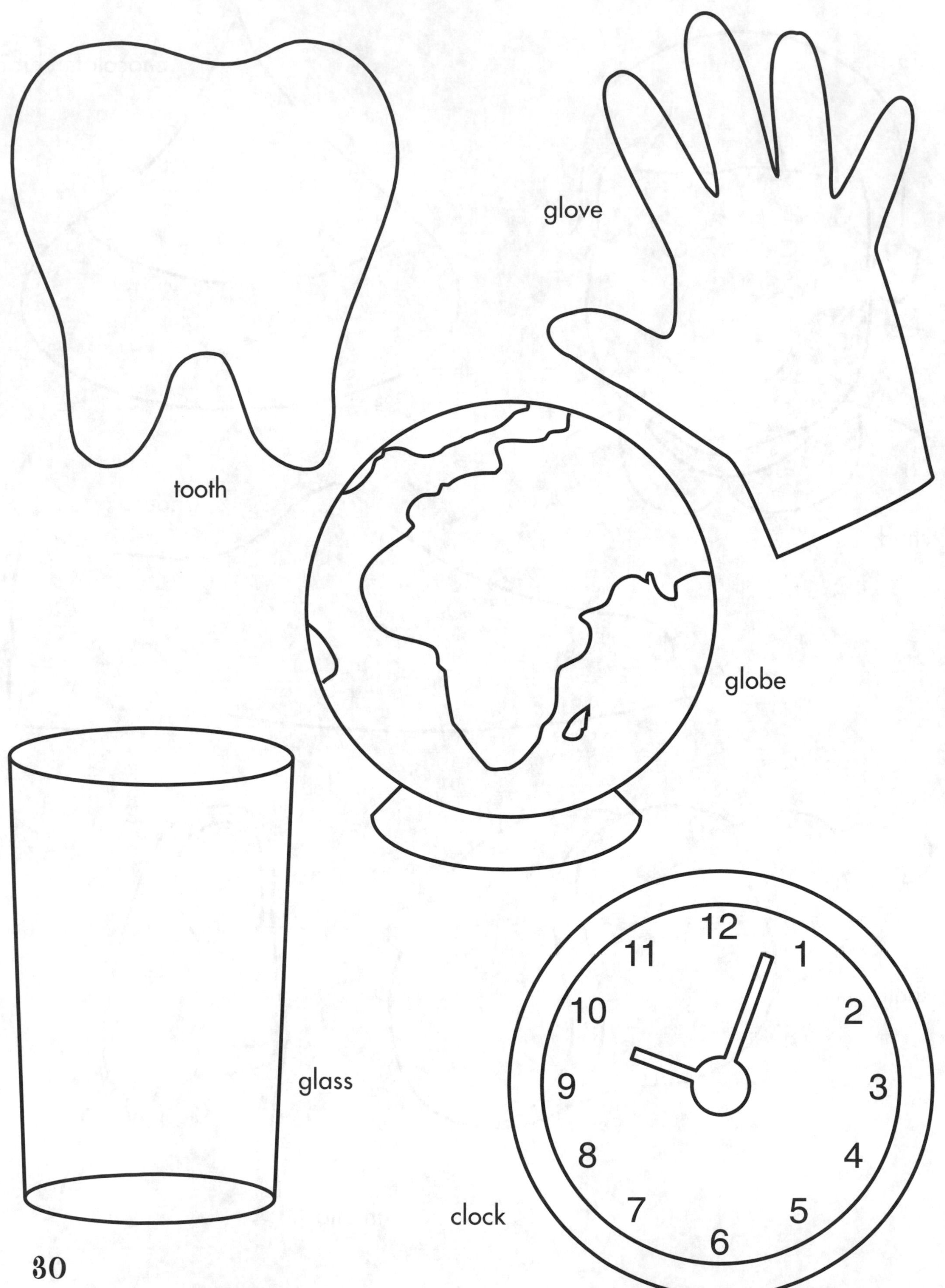
tooth
glove
globe
glass
clock
12
1
2
3
4
5
6
7
8
9
10
11

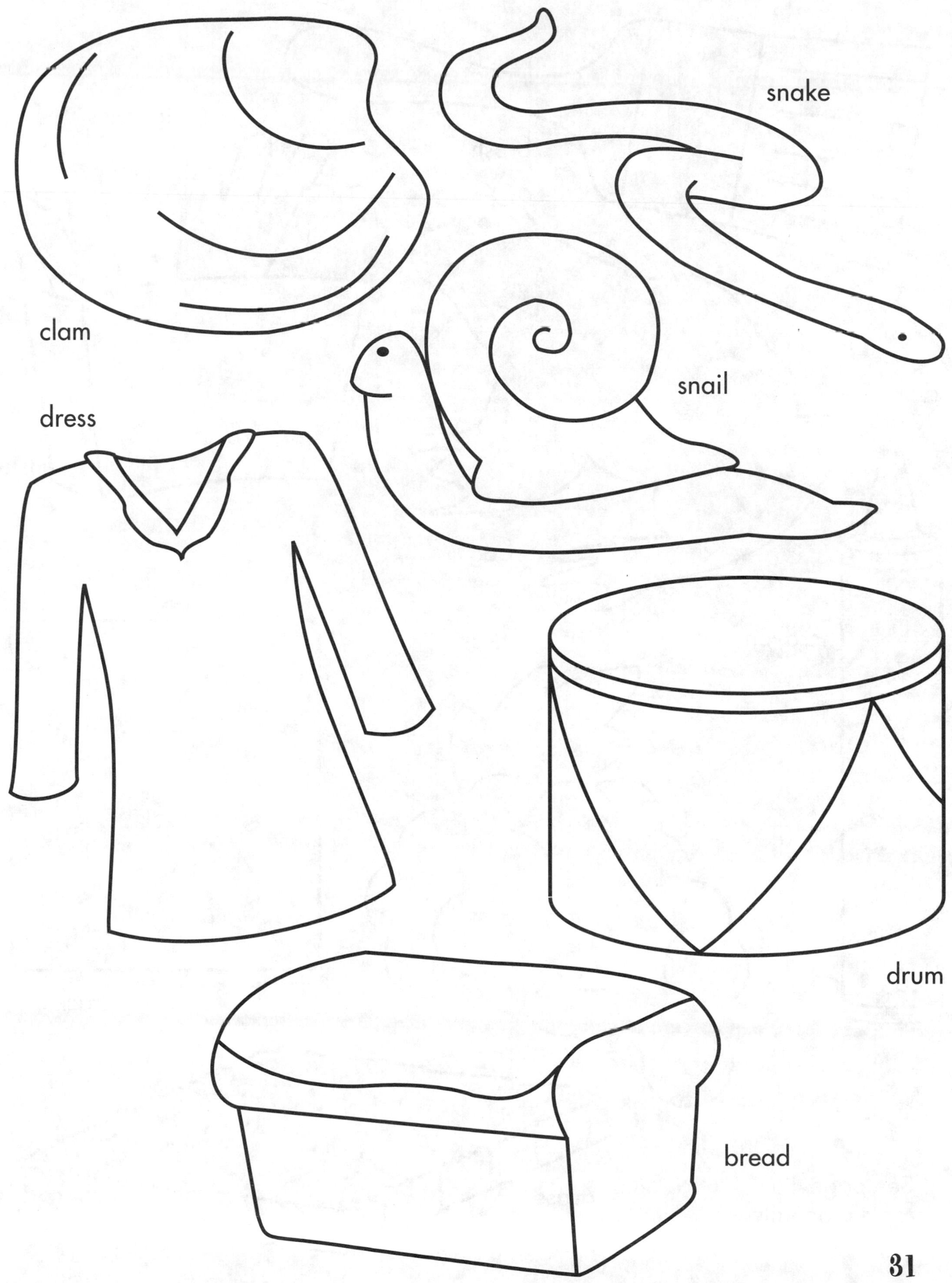
snake
clam
snail
dress
drum
bread

Consonant Blends and Digraphs

See page 16
for a crocodile.

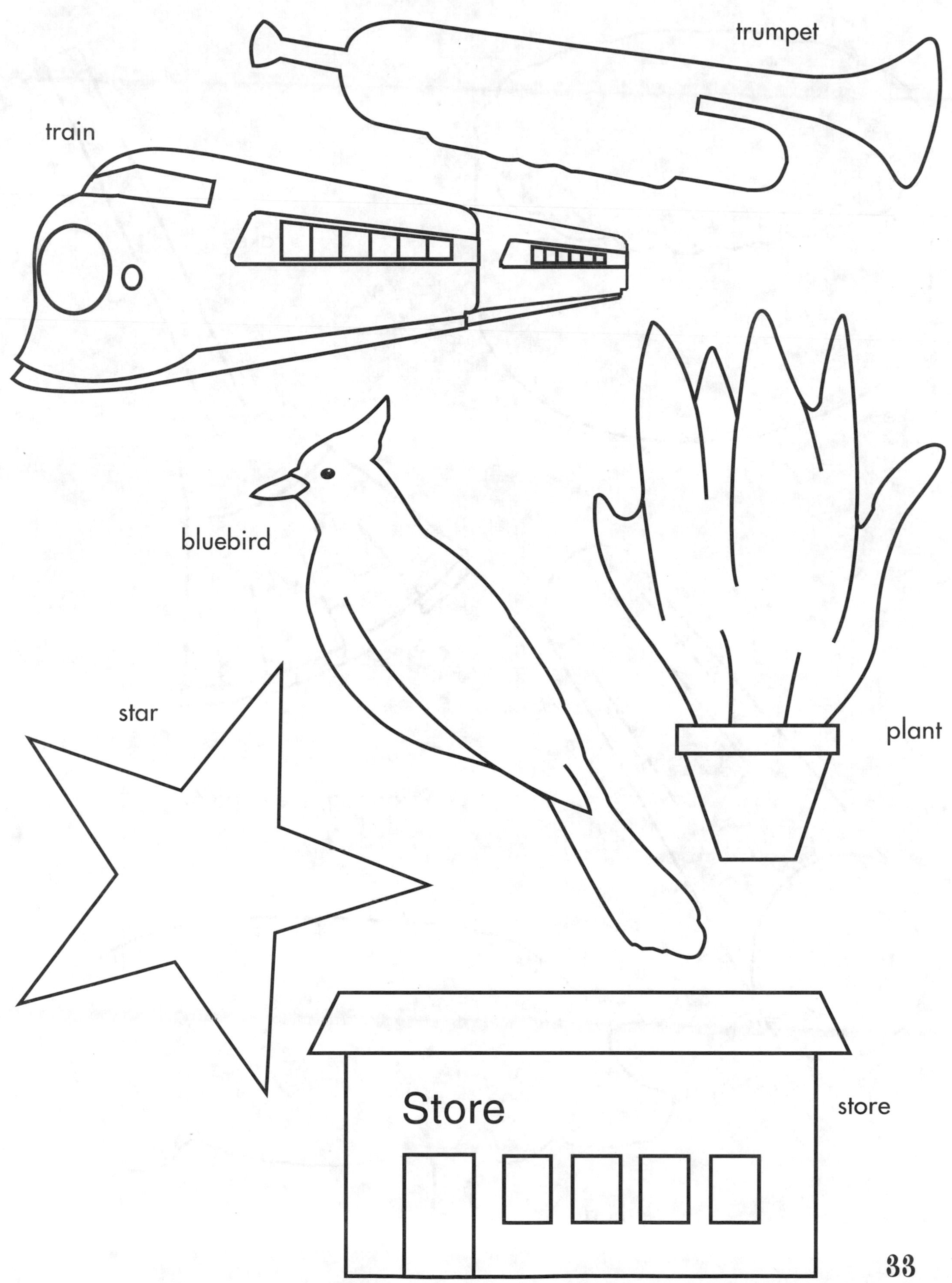
trumpet
train
bluebird
plant
star
Store
store

Rhyme Sort: Words in the Woods

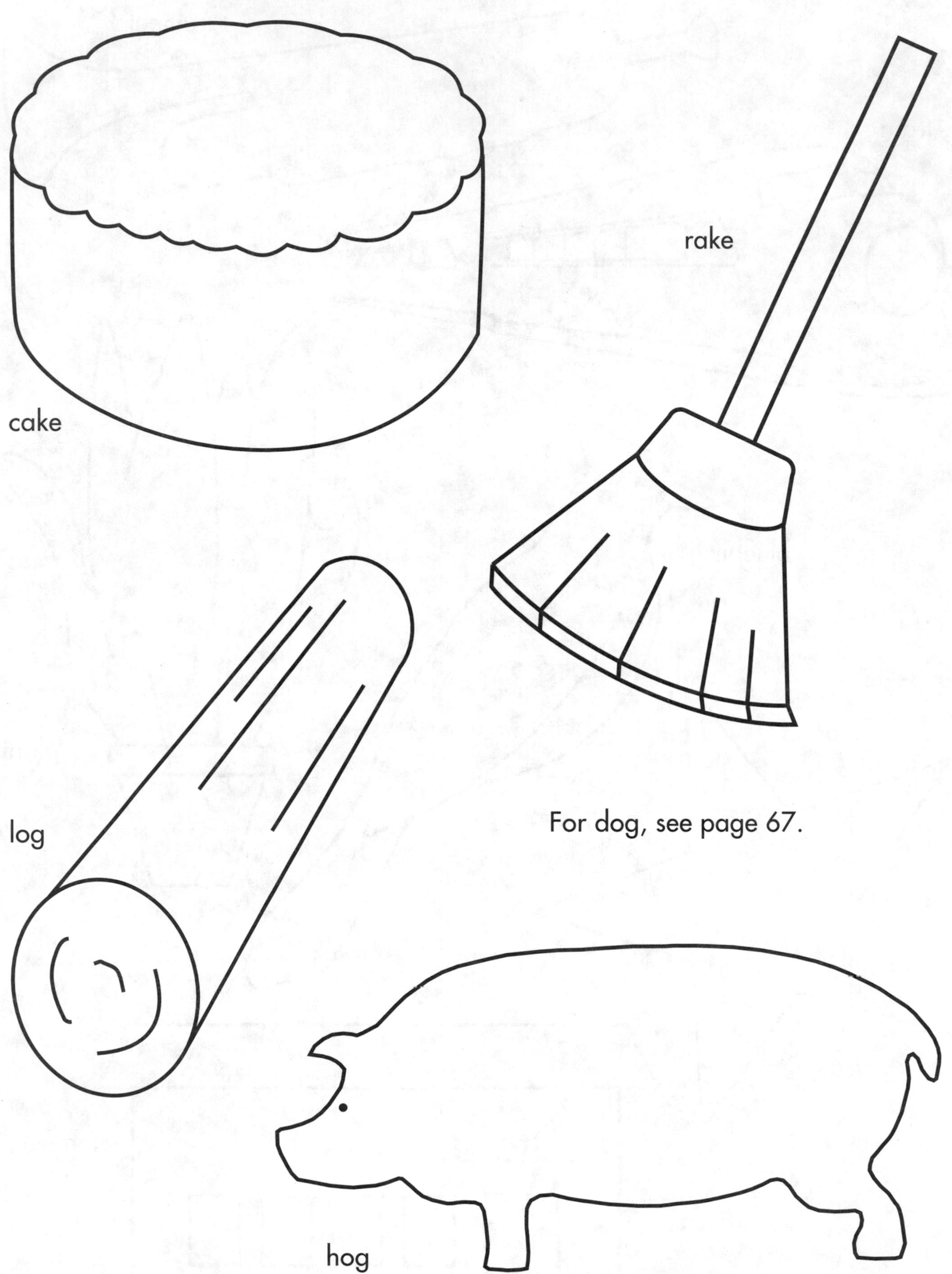

For dog, see page 67.

Rhyme Sort: Words in the Woods

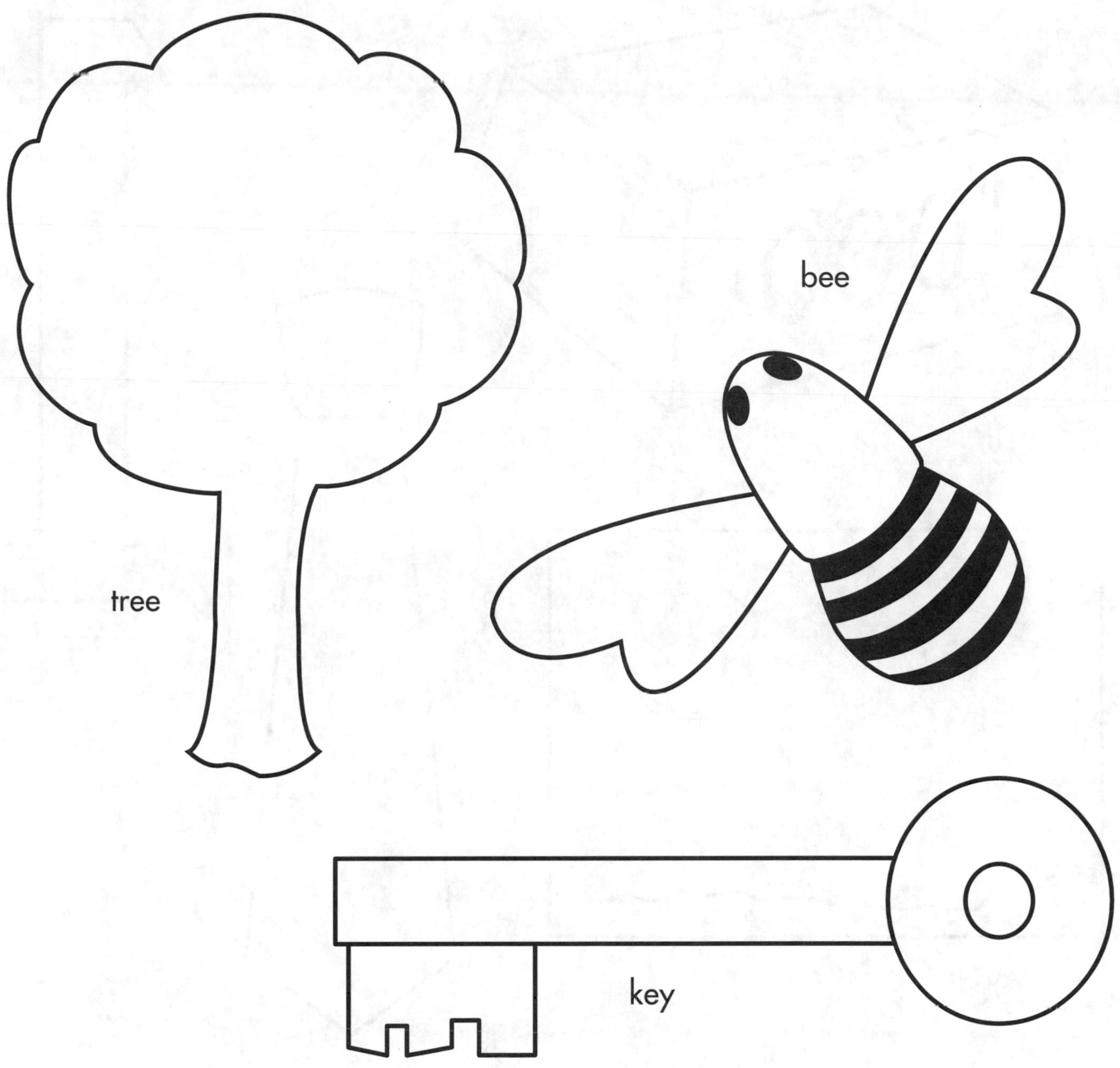

Rhyme Sort: Sky Words

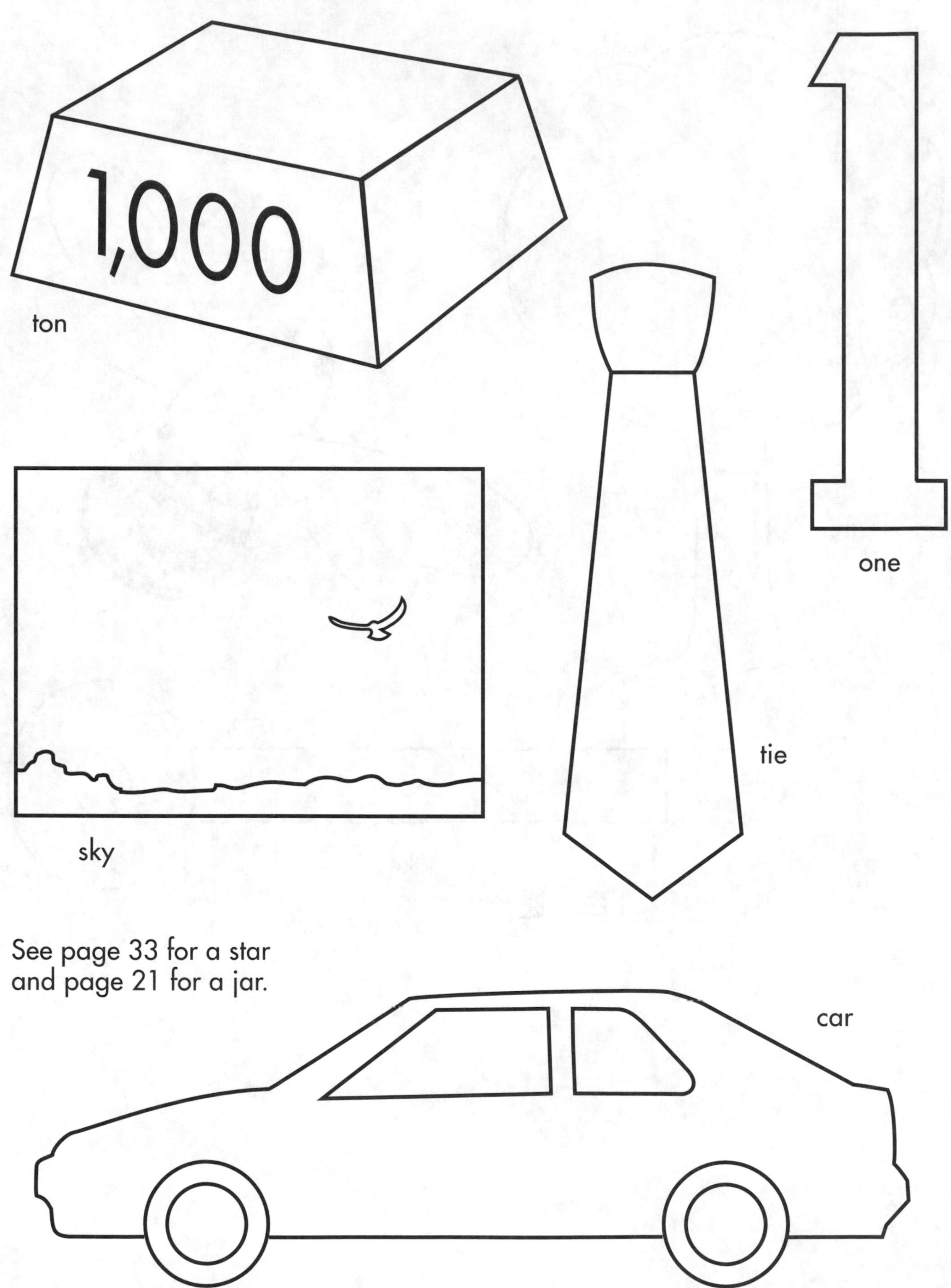

See page 33 for a star
and page 21 for a jar.

Rhyme Sort: Sky Words

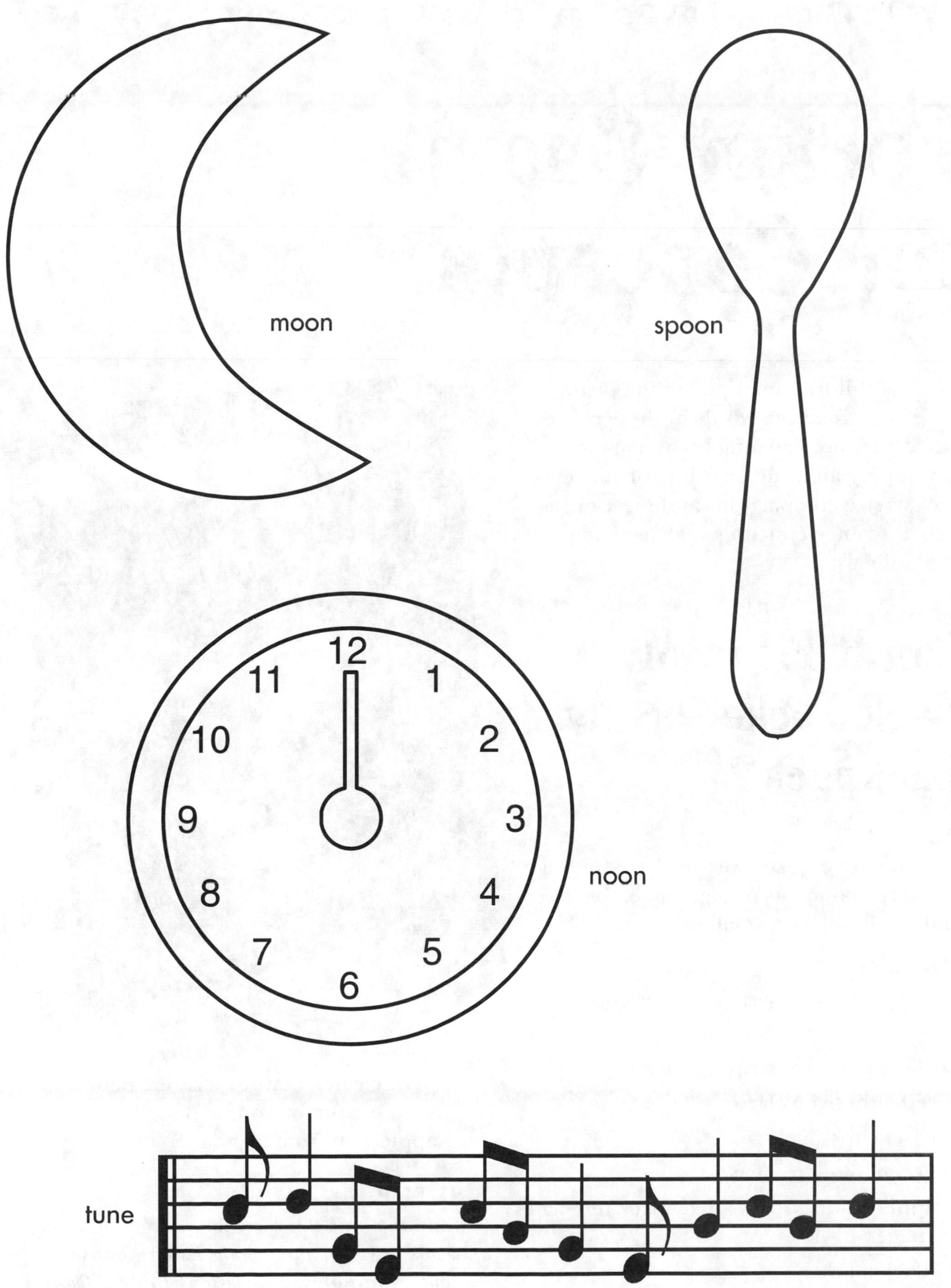

Pocket Charts for Concepts

As children manipulate the pictures and read the words in these charts, they are learning vocabulary and developing an understanding of concepts such as size comparisons and location, as well as science concepts such as shadows and animals.

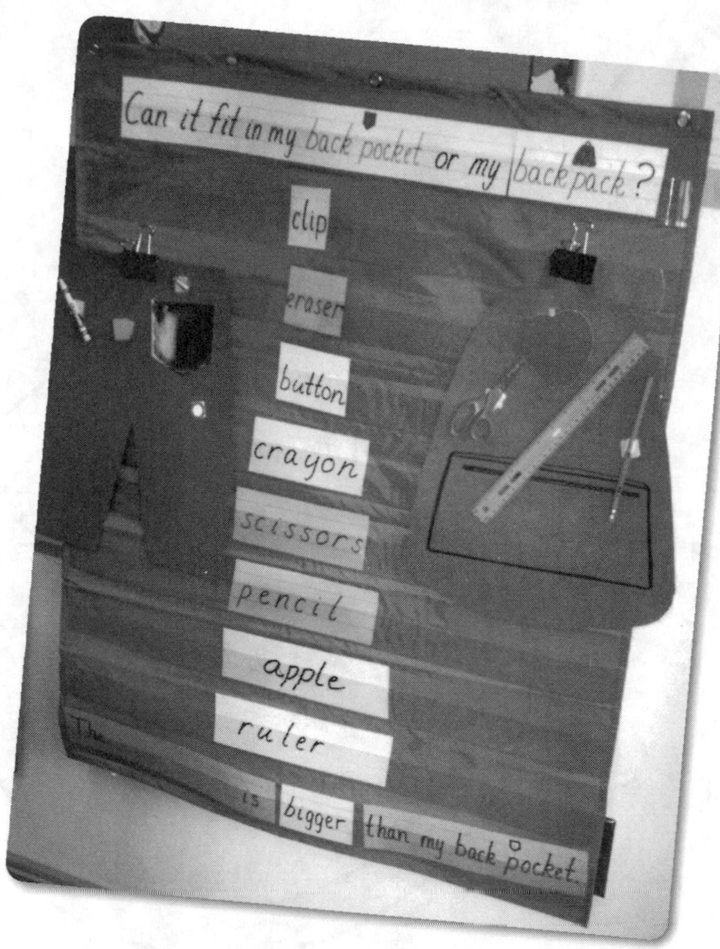

Can It Fit in My Back Pocket or My Backpack?

PURPOSE

To compare objects; sort by size; and learn about the concepts of big, bigger, biggest and small, smaller, smallest.

MATERIALS

- 34" x 42" pocket chart or 42" x 58" pocket chart
- 10-12 sentence strips in various colors
- self-adhesive Velcro
- easel clips
- green, blue, red tag
- apple, pants, pocket, backpack templates (pages 46–49)
- black marker
- scissors
- plastic ruler, crayon, scissors, pencil, small eraser, button, paper clip, apple (cut from tagboard)

SETUP

You can set up this chart for each lesson, change words as you go through the lessons, or use a double chart and set up lessons 1 and 2 together.

POCKET CHART WORDS

Can it fit in my back pocket or my backpack?

My back pocket is _______

My backpack is _______

The _______ is the

The _______ is

than my back pocket

than my backpack

clip, eraser, button, crayon, scissors, pencil, apple, ruler

big, bigger, biggest, small, smaller, smallest

(*See photos.*)

1 Trace and cut pants, pocket, apple, and backpack from tagboard. Glue pocket to pants.

2 Attach one side of self-adhesive Velcro on pants and backpack. Attach the other side to the items.

3 Attach pants and backpack to chart with easel clips.

4 Write words on sentence strips. Increase size of strips for each object word. Use rebus style for the sentence, "Can it fit in my back pocket or backpack?" (See photo left.)

Lesson 1: Sort by Size

1 Explain to children that you are going to sort some school items by deciding where to store various items—a back pocket or a backpack. Establish that everything will fit in the backpack, but a backpack is so big, small items might get lost in it. Additionally, you want to know what could fit in their back pocket.

2 Read the word and show the corresponding object. Ask children which is the best place for each of the objects.

3 Hand an object to a child and have him or her attach the object to either the pocket or the backpack. Place word in chart. Continue until you've used all the objects and words.

4 Then have children arrange the sentence strip words in size order (see photo on page 38).

Lesson 2: Big, bigger, biggest. . . small, smaller, smallest

1 Place the sentences for comparing size in chart.

2 Discuss with children the relative size of each object. Ask which is the biggest object, smallest object, etc. Arrange the objects and words in size order in or near the chart depending on which size chart you are using.

3 Read and complete the sentences correctly with the children.

4 The lesson can be repeated with various comparisons and word choices.

5 Set the chart up for children to use alone or in pairs.

ESL Variations

1 Hold up each object. Describe how the objects are used and the characteristics of each.

2 Have students point out the object and then give each item to the teacher or another student.

3 Ask questions like:
Is this the paper clip?
Is this the paper clip or the ruler?
What is this?

4 To help with the sorting activity write the words *small* and *big* on sentence strips. Place on floor or table. Have the children sort the objects. Then increase the difficulty by changing the words to *small, smaller, smallest* and *big, bigger, biggest.*

5 Ask questions like:
Which is smaller? bigger?, and so on.
Then continue with:
Can it fit in my back pocket?

Literature Integrations

Blue Sea by Robert Kalan. Greenwillow, 1979.

Too Much by Dorothy Stott. Penguin, 1990.

Biggest, Strongest, Fastest by Steve Jenkins. Houghton Mifflin, 1995.

Who's in That Tree?

PURPOSE

To discover that each of these animals is likely to be found near or in a tree in their own special home.

MATERIALS

- 6 sentence strips of various colors
- permanent marker
- scissors
- green, brown, white tagboard
- crayons, glue
- fish, rabbit, spider, bee, owl, and tree templates (pages 50–52)
- self-adhesive Velcro

SETUP

1 Use a different color for each line of the poem. Lines one and two should be the same color.

POCKET CHART WORDS

"Who's in that tree?"
(poem by Valerie SchifferDanoff)

Who's in that tree?
Who can it be?
I'm a fish in the pond. It can't be me.
I'm a rabbit in a hole. It can't be me.
I'm a spider on a web. It can't be me.
I'm a bee in a hive. It can't be me.
Whoo. I'm an owl. Now can you see?

2 Trace and cut treetop and trunk. (Note: This is the same tree used for Whisky Frisky on page 96.)

3 Copy, color, cut, and glue animals to white tagboard.

4 Attach one side of Velcro to the tree, the other side to the animals.

5 Place tree in chart. Secure with push pins or hang tree with easel clips.

6 Place sentence strips in chart.

7 Discuss with children all the animals that could be in, on, or near a tree. Read the poem, attaching the animals to chart. Children will love repeating the poem. Take turns matching the animals to the words and attaching them to the chart.

Variations

1 Make separate animal name cards for the animals in the poem and use them for a picture/name match activity.

2 Generate a list of other animals (for example, an ant, a bird, or a squirrel) that can be in, on, or near a tree. Discuss where they are likely to be found.

3 Have children draw a tree and the animals.

4 Create a tree mural with paints or craft paper. Have children draw animals, and then cut and glue them to the painted tree. Write animal words on sentence strips and glue them to the mural.

5 Take the class for a walk in a park so they can see firsthand what animals are in, on, or near a tree.

ESL Variations

1 To reinforce students' understanding of location words and animals names, ask questions like:

Is the owl on the tree?

Is the owl near the spider web?

Then increase the difficulty of the questions you ask:

Is the fish in a hole or in a pond?

Where is the rabbit?

2 Invent riddles such as:

I have long ears. I have a short tail. I hop.

I live in a hole. Who am I?

Literature Integrations

Red Leaf, Yellow Leaf by Lois Ehlert. Harcourt Brace Jovanovich, 1991.

Once There Was A Tree by Natalia Romanova. Penguin, 1985.

Me and My Shadow

PURPOSE

To experience poetry, learn rhyming words, and develop an understanding of shadows.

MATERIALS

- 34" x 42" pocket chart
- 2 orange, 3 blue, 4 yellow sentence strips
- person/shadow templates (page 53)
- construction paper (Tru-Ray is best) or 4-ply tag in black for shadows, and colors (could use multicultural paper) for person
- marker, scissors, and glue

SETUP

1. Copy, color, and glue onto tagboard 4 people, 4 shadows, and 1 longer shadow. You can also trace and cut the templates from construction paper.
2. Glue shadows onto people to show side, front, bigger than (that shadow template is elongated). Do not glue the extra shadow and person. You can use them to demonstrate how shadows move.
3. Write poem on three different color sentence strips. "Look, look" on orange, "What do I see?" on blue, and shadow sentences on yellow. Cut orange and blue strips to size.
4. Place poem and people/shadows in chart correctly.
5. Introduce the chart by discussing what a shadow is. Explain that a shadow is a dark area created when the sun or light shines on a person or object. Shadows occur because light cannot shine through the person or object. A shadow moves and grows depending on the location of the sun or light. Use the extra person and shadow to show how a shadow moves.
6. Read poem with children.
7. Pair children and have each pair act out the poem by pretending to be the children and the shadows.

POCKET CHART WORDS

"Me and My Shadow"
(poem by Valerie SchifferDanoff)

Look, look!
What do I see?
It's my shadow in front of me.
Look, look!
What do I see?
It's my shadow next to me.
Look, look!
What do I see?
Now my shadow is bigger than me.
Look, look!
What do I see?
Only my heels in back of me.

Variations

1 Children might enjoy drawing or tracing one another's shadow.

2 Darken the room and shine a flashlight or go outside in the sunshine for a hands-on experience of shadows.

3 Make shadow portraits of each child using a projector.

Literature Integrations

What Makes a Shadow? by Robert Bulla. HarperCollins, 1962, 1994.

Will Spring Ever Come to Gobbler's Knob? by Julia Spencer Moutran, Ph.D. Literary Publications, 1992.

It's Groundhog Day! by Steven Kroll. Holiday House, 1987.

Over, Under, In, On, Through

PURPOSE

To distinguish among the concepts of and learn the correct vocabulary use for the words *over, under, in, on, through.*

MATERIALS

- 8 sentence strips of various colors
- black permanent marker
- scissors
- crayons
- marker
- glue
- white tagboard
- car, blanket, puddle, horse, house, and children templates (pages 54–55)

SETUP

1 Write words on sentence strips. Put each sentence on a different color strip.

2 Copy the children, horse, puddle, car, blanket, and house templates. Color and glue onto white tagboard. Then cut around shape. Cut car door on dotted line so it opens.

POCKET CHART WORDS

(poem by Valerie SchifferDanoff)

Over and under, in, on, through
That is what I like to do.
Jumping over puddles, yoo-hoo!
Hide under my blanket, peek-a-boo!
Go in a car, toodle-oo
Ride on a horse, whoop-de-do!
Look through a window, I see you!
Over and under, in, on, through!

3 Place poem in chart and read with children. Put correct representative pictures in the chart as you read. Read slowly using the pictures to help explain the concepts.

4 Remove the pictures from the chart. Read the poem again. Ask children to match pictures correctly.

Variations

1 Write the words, *over, under, in, on, through* on white sentence strips. Have the children match these words to the words in chart.

2 Generate a list of more possibilities for *over, under, in, on, through.* For example, *under* a bridge, *in* the school bus, *on* the swings, and so on.

ESL Variations

1 First ask questions that can be answered with yes/no.

Is the girl in the car?
Is the boy under the blanket?

2 Then ask questions that require a more complex response such as either/or questions or ones that use the vocabulary developed by the chart such as *under, in, over, on, through.*

Is the boy jumping over or under the puddle?

Where is the boy?

Who is under the blanket?

3 Have students demonstrate actions.

Put the boy in the car.

Next put the boy under the blanket.

Literature Integration

Wheel Away by Dayle Ann Dodds. Harper and Row, 1989.

These Eggs Are Talking

PURPOSE

To reinforce recognition of color words and to learn about animals that hatch from eggs.

MATERIALS

- 34" x 42" pocket chart
- 12 white sentence strips
- 2 green sentence strips
- black, green, orange, purple, blue, yellow markers
- plastic eggs, available in party shops
- plastic animals that will fit in eggs or small animal pictures
- tagboard

POCKET CHART WORDS

These eggs are talking.
Read the clues. Open the eggs.
Match the colors to the clues.

octopus, starfish, chick, turtle

pink, blue, yellow, purple

I will grow up to be a rooster or hen.

I am the _____ in the _____ egg.

I twinkle in the sea not in the sky.

I am the _____ in the _____ egg.

I need all of my arms to open a clam.

I am the _____ in the _____ egg.

SETUP

1 Write sentences on the white sentence strips and place in chart. Write the "color" word on white sentence strip cards with matching markers. (E.g., blue with a blue marker; yellow with a yellow marker.) Place these cards near the chart. On green sentence strips write the names of the animals.

2 Fill plastic eggs with various plastic animals or pictures of the animals. Place the eggs in a basket near the chart.

Note: do not use small plastic animals with preschool children unless supervised by an adult.

3 Have children take turns opening eggs and matching the plastic animals to the animal word cards. Then have them match the "color" cards to the eggs. Insert both cards in the correct sentence strip in the chart.

4 Children can work as a class, in pairs, or independently to open the eggs and place correct words in chart.

Variation

Change clues and egg contents. Some additional possibilities are:

Q. My shell is harder than an egg shell.

A. turtle

Q. I have a very long tail, a big jaw, sharp teeth, and I'm green.

A. alligator

Q. I have a fin, sharp teeth, and I live in the ocean.

A. shark

Q. I begin life as a tadpole.

A. frog

A. I can turn my head all the way around.

A. owl

ESL Variation

Use this chart to give students exposure to present and future tenses—without using the terms. For example:

Now I am a chick. I will grow up to be a rooster or a hen.

I begin life as a tadpole. I will grow up to be a frog.

I start life in an egg. I will grow up to be a. . .

Literature Integrations

Chickens Aren't the Only Ones by Ruth Heller. Scholastic, 1981.

The Egg by Gallimard Jeunesse and Pascale de Bourgoing. Scholastic, 1992.

Tap! Tap! the egg cracked. . . by Keith Faulkner. Marboro Books, 1992.

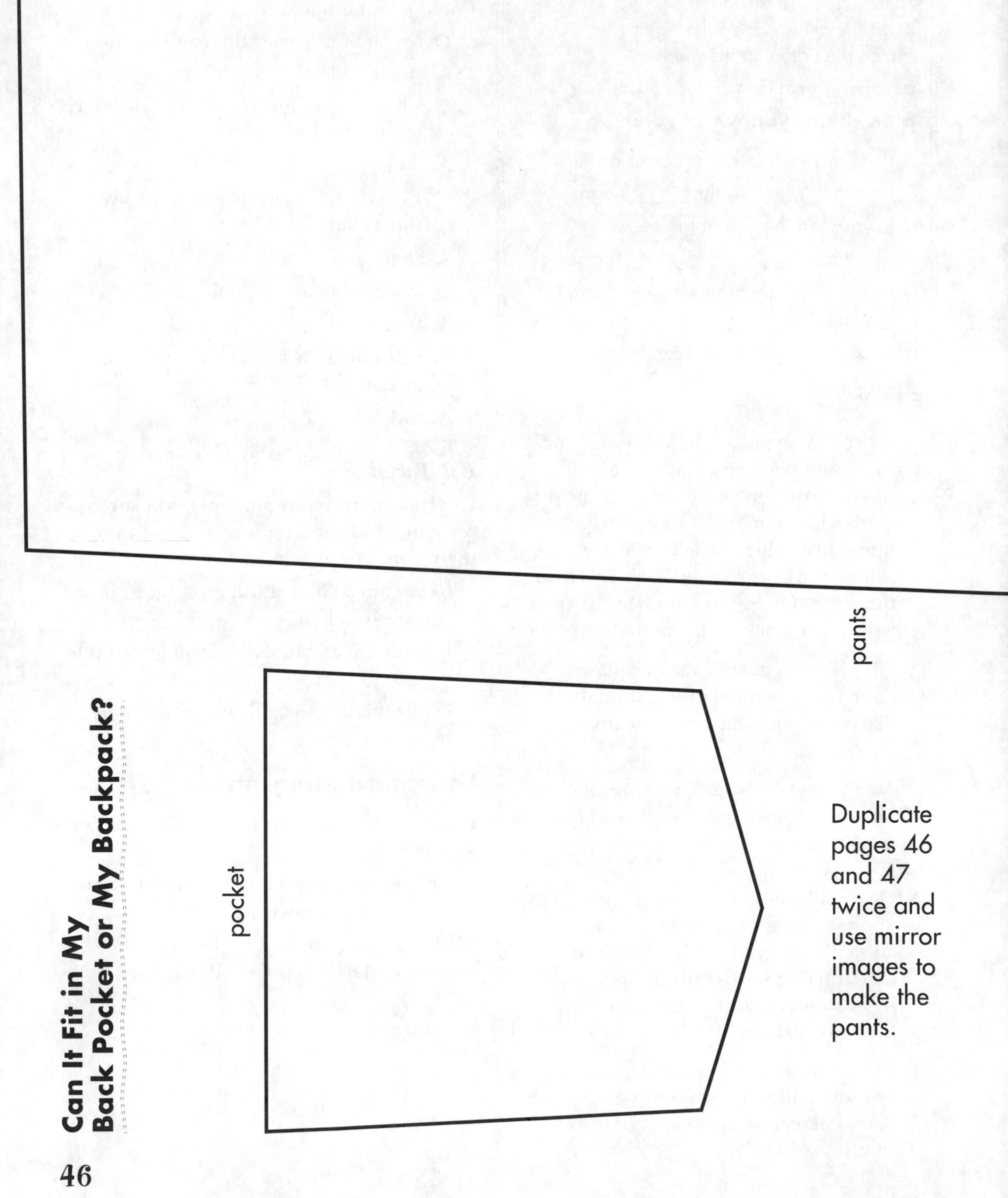

Duplicate pages 46 and 47 twice and use mirror images to make the pants.

pants

Can It Fit in My Back Pocket or My Backpack?

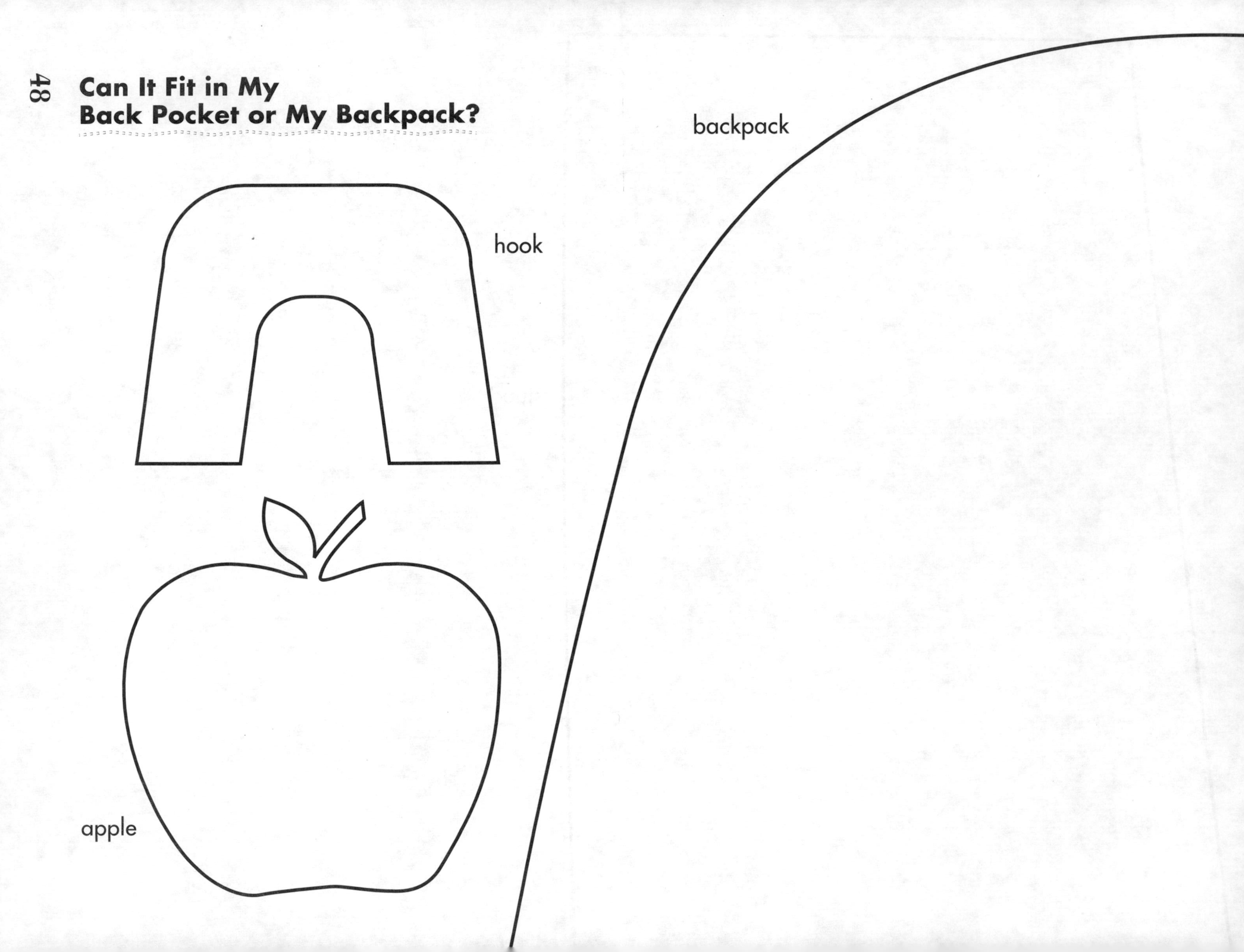

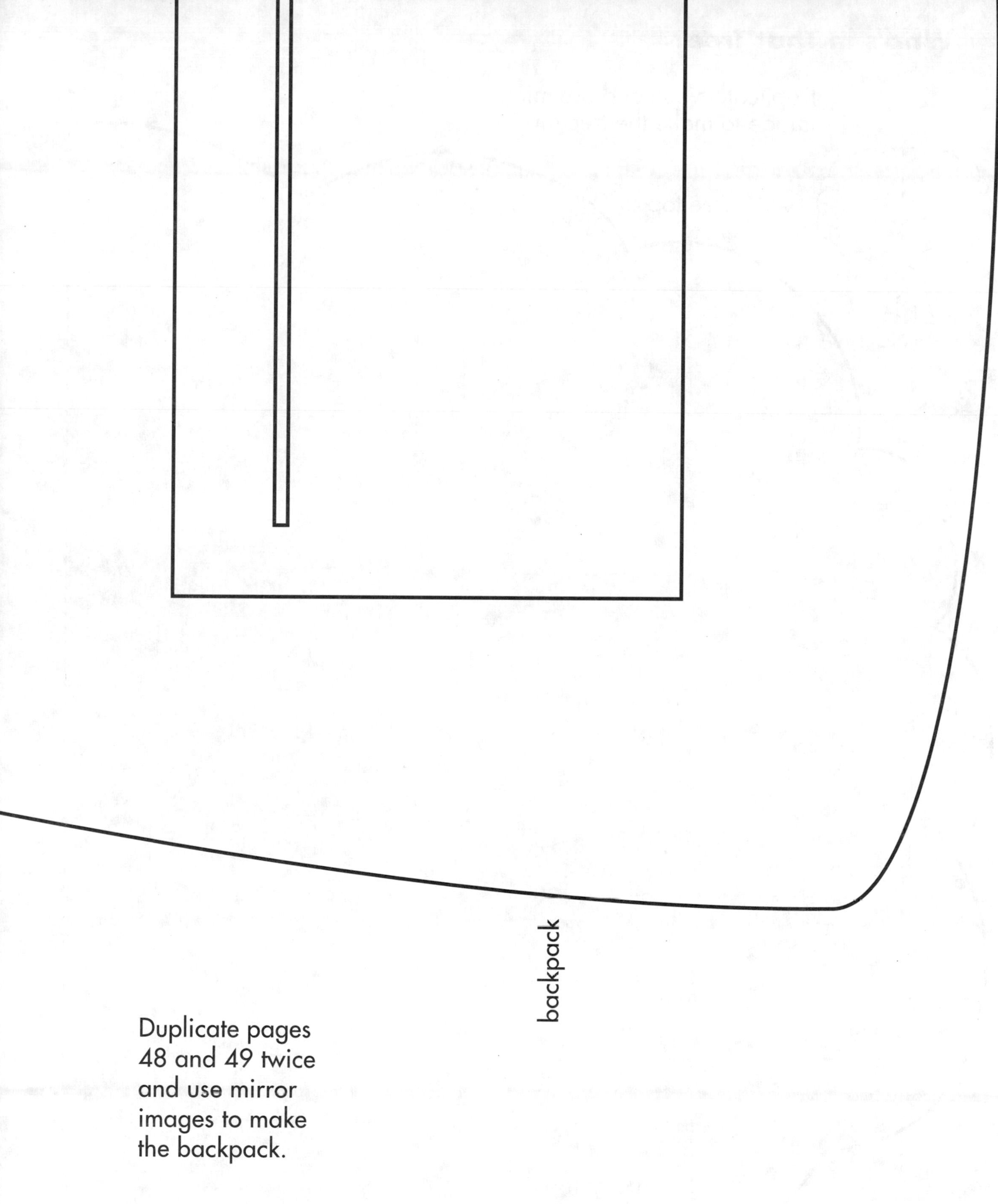

Duplicate pages 48 and 49 twice and use mirror images to make the backpack.

Who's in That Tree?

Duplicate twice and use mirror image to make the tree top.

Who's in That Tree?

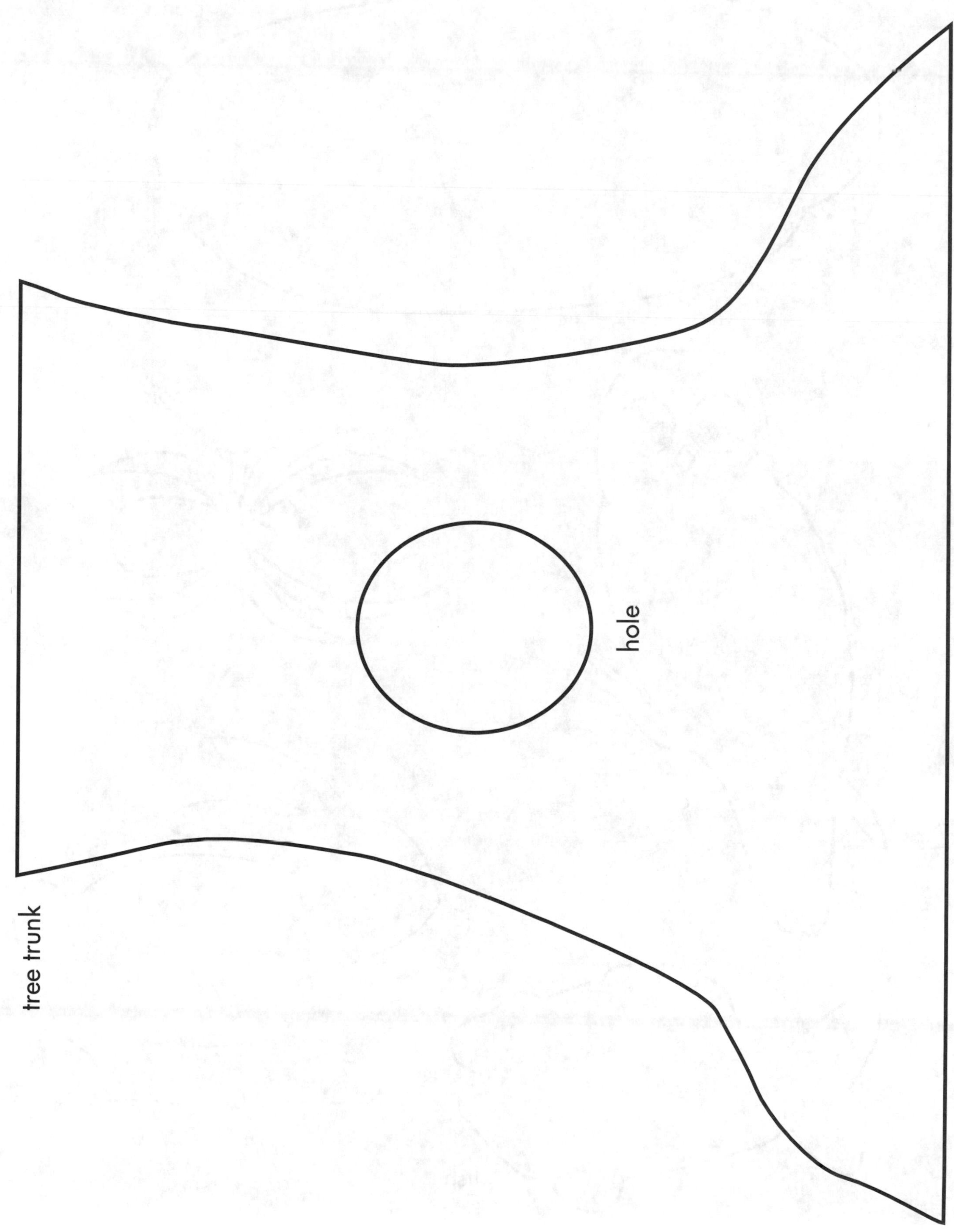

Who's in That Tree?

Me and My Shadow

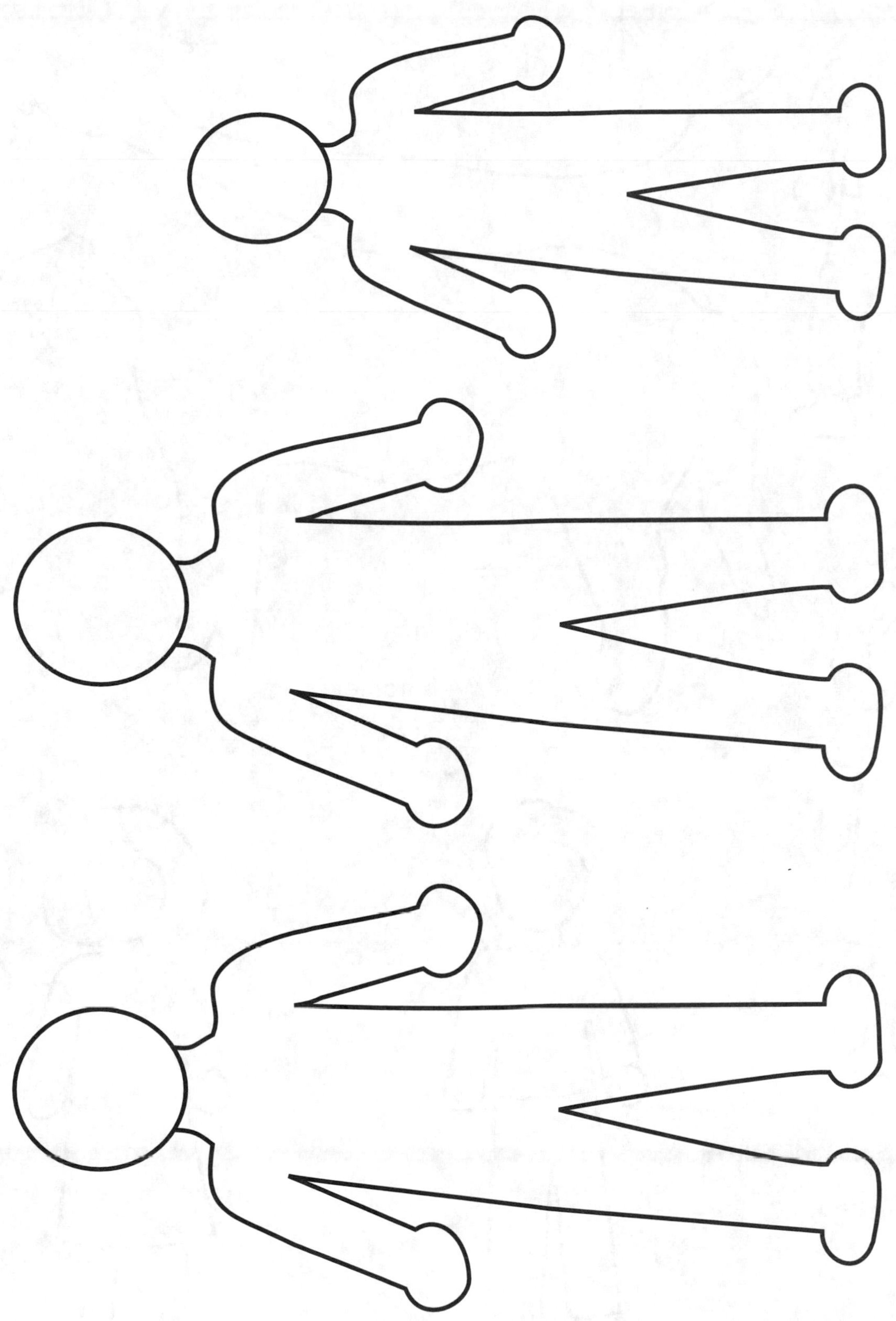

puddle
boy
horse
girl
person
person

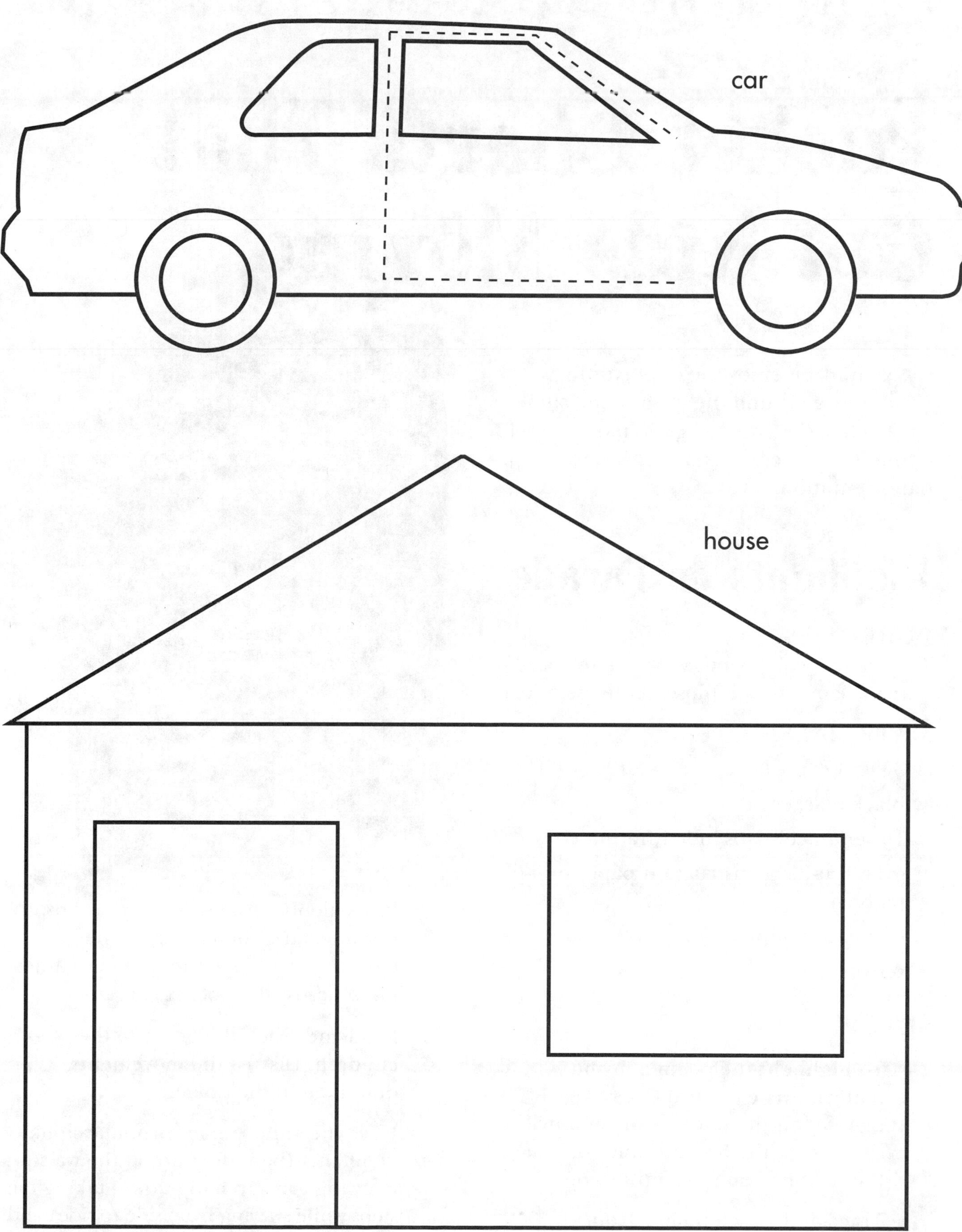
car
house

Pocket Charts That Get Kids Moving

Children enjoy the opportunity to move around the classroom. These charts encourage gross motor development and increase students' sense of spatial orientation.

Elephants on Parade

PURPOSE

To imitate an elephant's walk and to coordinate movements with those of other students.

MATERIALS

- 34" x 42" pocket chart
- black marker
- 10 sentence strips in 5 different colors
- gray Tru-Ray construction paper or 4-ply tagboard
- elephant template (page 62)
- scissors

SETUP

1. To highlight the poem's rhyme pattern, write the two lines of each couplet on the same color sentence strips, e.g., the first two lines on blue, the next two on pink, and so on.
2. Trace and cut elephants from templates.
3. Place elephants and sentence strips in pocket chart. You can make the elephants look like they are marching up or across the pocket chart.
4. Read and teach the poem to the children. Discuss the movements described in the poem.
5. Have the children, in turn, march like elephants (bend forward at the waist, allowing arms to hang down, taking big steps while swaying from side to side) and mimic what each elephant is doing.

6 Divide class into groups of five. Assign one of the five actions in the poem to each member of the group. Have them practice the action, e.g., swinging "trunk," waving flag, and so forth, so their movements are synchronized.

7 Have the children march in lines of five to act out the poem.

POCKET CHART WORDS

Five gray elephants marching through a glade.

Decide to stop and play at having a parade.

The first one swings his trunk and announces he'll lead.

The next waves a flag which of course they need.

The third gray elephant trumpets a song.

The fourth beats a drum as he marches along.

While the fifth makes believe he's the whole show.

And nods and smiles to the crowd as they go.

Five gray elephants marching through the glade.

Have a lot of fun during their parade.

Variation
Have students suggest other animals and possible movements to create a variation on the poem.

Literature Integrations

17 Kings and 42 Elephants by Margaret Mahy. Penguin, 1972, 1987.

Elephant by Judy Allen. Walker Books, Ltd. 1992.

Teddy Bear, Teddy Bear

PURPOSE
To practice various body movements on command.

MATERIALS
- 34" x 42" pocket chart
- 4 sentence strips
- teddy bear templates (pages 63–64)
- brown construction paper
- paper fasteners
- permanent marker
- scissors

SETUP

1 Write words on sentence strips and place in chart. Put one line on each strip.

POCKET CHART WORDS

Teddy bear, teddy bear turn around.
Teddy bear, teddy bear touch the ground.
Teddy bear, teddy bear jump up high.
Teddy bear, teddy bear touch the sky.

2 Trace, cut, and fasten a teddy bear together with paper fasteners and place in chart.

3 Show children how paper teddy moves and discuss how they can move.

4 Reread the poem. Have children move to the commands pretending to be the teddy bear.

Variations

1 Ask children what else a teddy bear can do and have them demonstrate the movement with the bear.

2 Add more commands to the teddy bear chart, for example:

Teddy bear, teddy bear touch your toes.

Teddy bear, teddy bear touch you nose.

Teddy bear, teddy bear hop around.

Teddy bear, teddy bear don't make a sound.

Teddy bear teddy bear touch your ear.

Teddy bear, teddy bear growl like a bear.

Teddy bear, teddy bear touch your knees.

Teddy bear, teddy bear buzz like bees.

3 You may wish to have children make their own teddy bears. See page 71 for this activity.

ESL Variation

1 Model the actions for students.

2 Ask students to perform increasingly more difficult series of actions. For example:

Touch your toes. Touch your toes first, then turn around.

Literature Integrations

Teddy Bear, Teddy Bear by Kathleen Hague. Scholastic, 1991.
Golden Bear by Ruth Young. Penguin, 1992.

Leaf, Leaf, Leaf

PURPOSE

To practice moving in slow motion like a leaf and to do and mime other actions such as falling, raking, and jumping.

MATERIALS

- 34" x 42" pocket chart
- 2 green sentence strips
- 3 orange sentence strips
- 2 blue sentence strips
- leaf templates (page 65)
- yellow, brown, orange 4- to 6-ply tagboard
- scissors
- permanent marker

SETUP

1 Write words on sentence strips. Place in chart to mimic leaves falling as shown. (You can also write the lines of the poem in green, orange, brown, and red markers on white sentence strips.)

2 Trace and cut about 12 leaves using templates and 4- to 6-ply tag. Place some leaves in chart and some leaves on the floor in front of the chart.

3. Read the words of the poem with the children.
4. Have children toss paper leaves up in the air to watch how they fall.
5. Have children read the poem and mimic the motion of the falling leaves.

POCKET CHART WORDS

Leaf, leaf, leaf
Fall, fall, falling
Leaves, leaves, leaves
Falling, falling, fall
Leaves, leaves, leaves
Rake, rake, raking
Leaves, leaves, leaves
Jumping! Jumping! Jump!

6. Have children act out the other action words in the poem.

Variations

1. You may wish to work on the "Raking the Leaves" activity at the same time. See page 69.
2. Ask children to describe other things they do with leaves. E.g., make a pile, mulch, use a leaf blower.
3. Go for a walk in a park, gather leaves, and make leaf rubbings by placing leaves under newsprint paper and going over with a crayon. Or, place a leaf between two sheets of wax paper and press with a warm iron. (You may want to enlist the help of a parent volunteer for this activity.)

Literature Integrations

Fresh Fall Leaves by Betsy Franco. Scholastic, 1994.

Free Fall by David Wiesner. William Morrow, 1988.

Six Little Snowflakes

PURPOSE

To have children move and still be aware of their surrounding space.

MATERIALS

- 34" x 42" pocket chart
- 4 blue sentence strips
- 2 white sentence strips
- snowflake templates (page 66)
- white tagboard
- glue
- scissors

SETUP

1 Write words on blue and white sentence strips alternating colors for each couplet.

2 Copy page of snowflakes to make as many snowflakes as desired. Glue to tagboard and cut around snowflake shape.

3 Place sentence strips and snowflakes in chart.

POCKET CHART WORDS

One little snowflake falls to the ground.
Two little snowflakes spin all around.
Three little snowflakes glitter and glow.
Four little snowflakes drift very slow.
Five little snowflakes fly away.
Six little snowflakes are here to stay.

4 Read over the poem with your class. Then have children take turns acting out the snowflake motions.

Variations

1 Point out the couplets to children. Ask children to tell you what other words rhyme with ending words for each couplet. Make a list.

2 Place poem in a double chart or use another pocket chart to make up simple addition and subtraction story problems based on the poem. Write these problems on sentence strips. Have children practice these problems together using snowflakes from the chart. For example:

Four snowflakes fall. Two more snowflakes fall. How many snowflakes are there all together? 4+2=6

Six snowflakes fall to the ground. Two snowflakes melt. How many snowflakes are left? 6-2=4

Literature Integrations

Wintertime by Ann Schweninger. Penguin, 1990.

Snow is Falling by Franklyn M. Branley. Harper & Row, 1986.

Six Snowy Sheep by Judith Ross and Stephanie Gordon Tessler. Penguin, 1995.

Animals

PURPOSE

To imitate the movements of various animals in order to develop smoother and more effective body movements and to increase students' sense of body consciousness.

MATERIALS

- 10 sentence strips in various colors.
- permanent marker
- scissors
- tagboard or construction paper
- animal templates (pages 52 and 67)

SETUP

1. Write words on sentence strips. Put one sentence on each colored strip.
2. Trace and cut animals from tagboard or construction paper.
3. Place words in pocket chart.

POCKET CHART WORDS

Animals

Can you hop like a rabbit?
Can you jump like a frog?
Can you walk like a duck?
Can you run like a dog?
Can you fly like a bird?
Can you swim like a fish?
And be still like a good child—
As still as this?

4. Read poem with children.
5. Ask children to place animals in chart to match the words.
6. Have children imitate animal movements as the poem is read again.

Variation

Ask children to tell you other things these animals can do. Write their replies on sentence strips. Cut to size and place in bottom pocket of chart. Reread the poem. Have children come up and match the words to the various animals. Then have the children act out these new movements.

ESL Variation

Use this pocket chart to teach comparison and vocabulary.

Literature Integrations

Pretend You're a Cat by Jean Marzollo. Penguin, 1990.

Just Me by Marie Hall Ets. Penguin, 1978.

In the Forest by Marie Hall Ets. Penguin, 1944, 1972.

Elephants on Parade

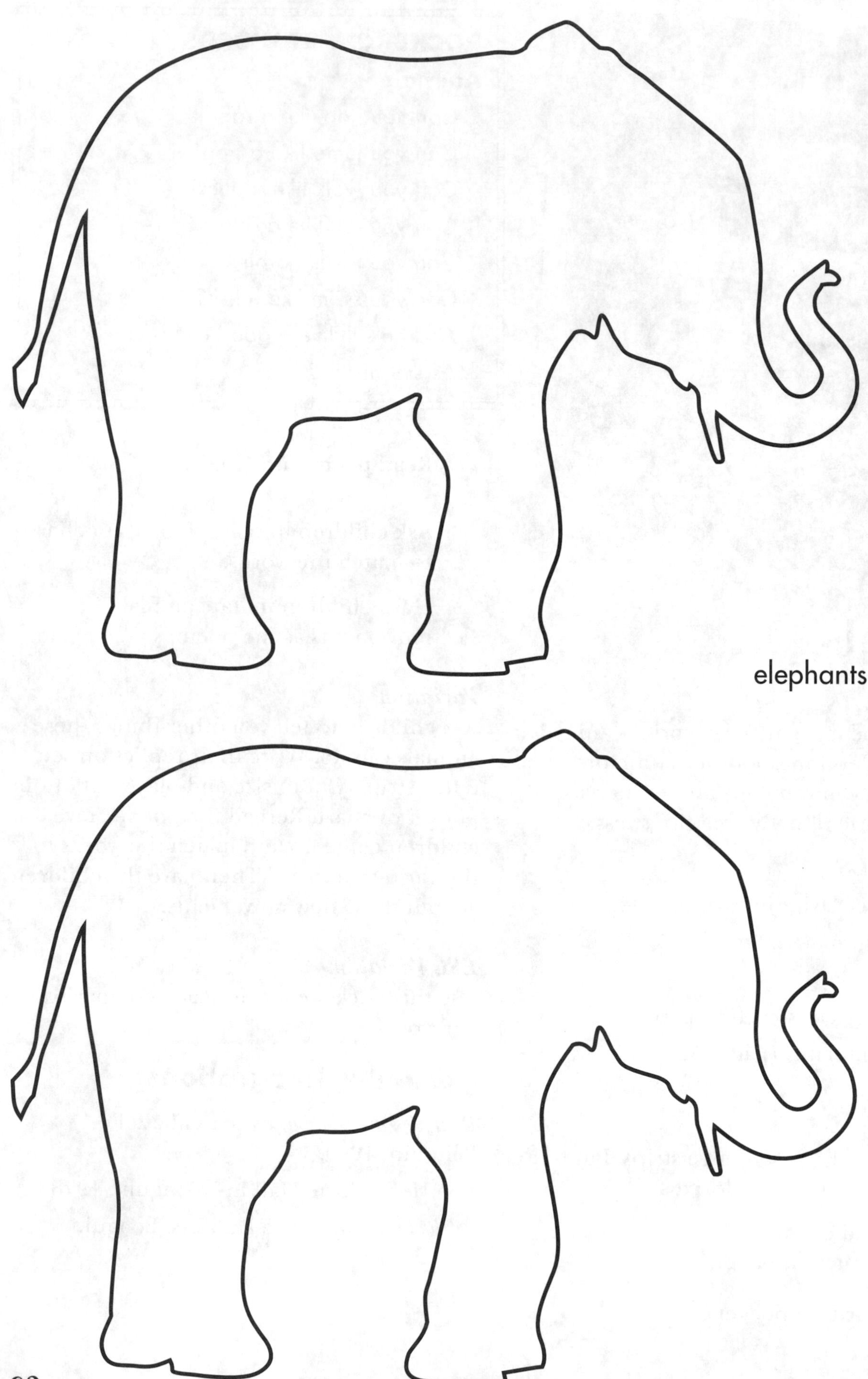

elephants

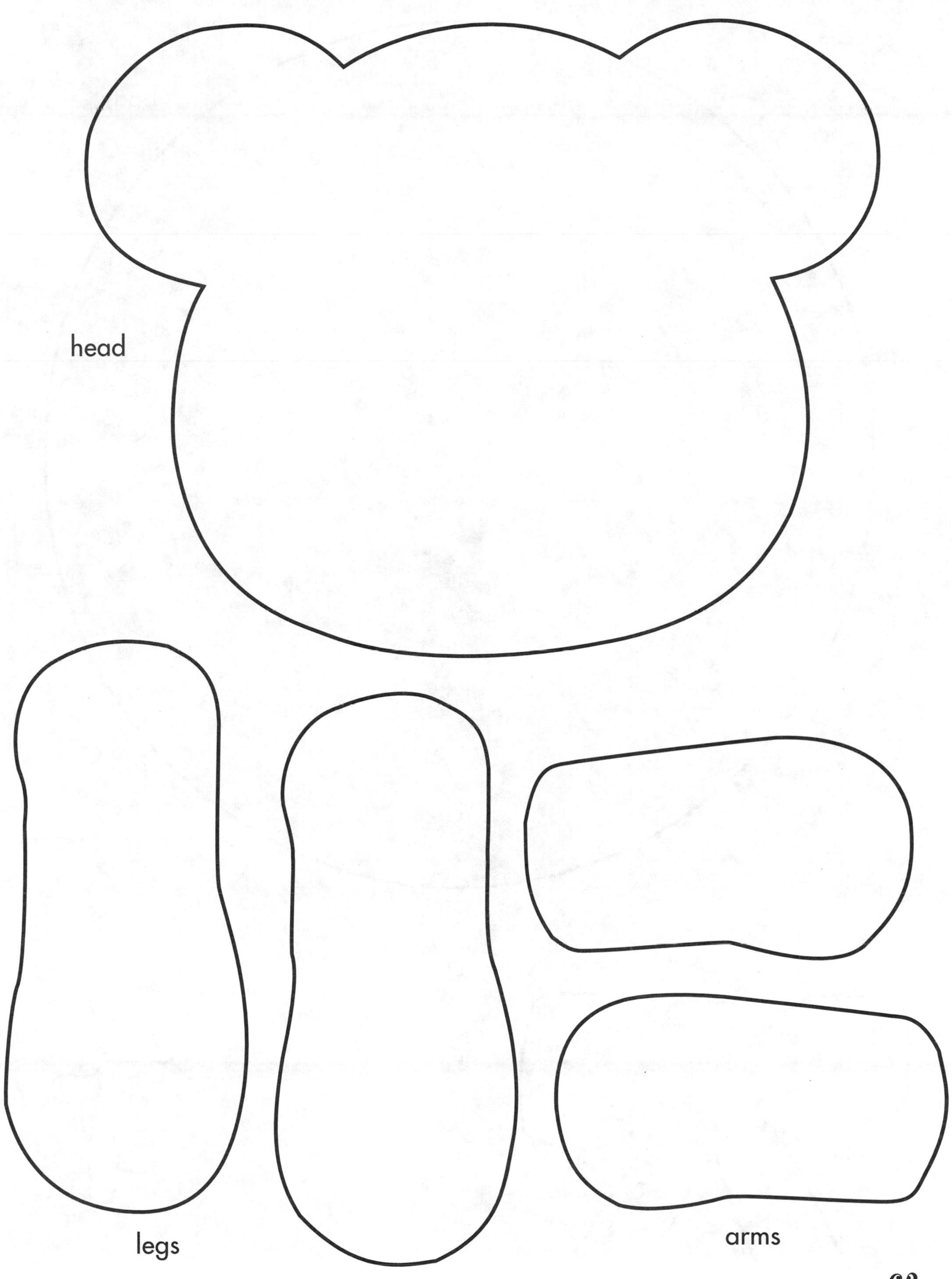
head
legs
arms

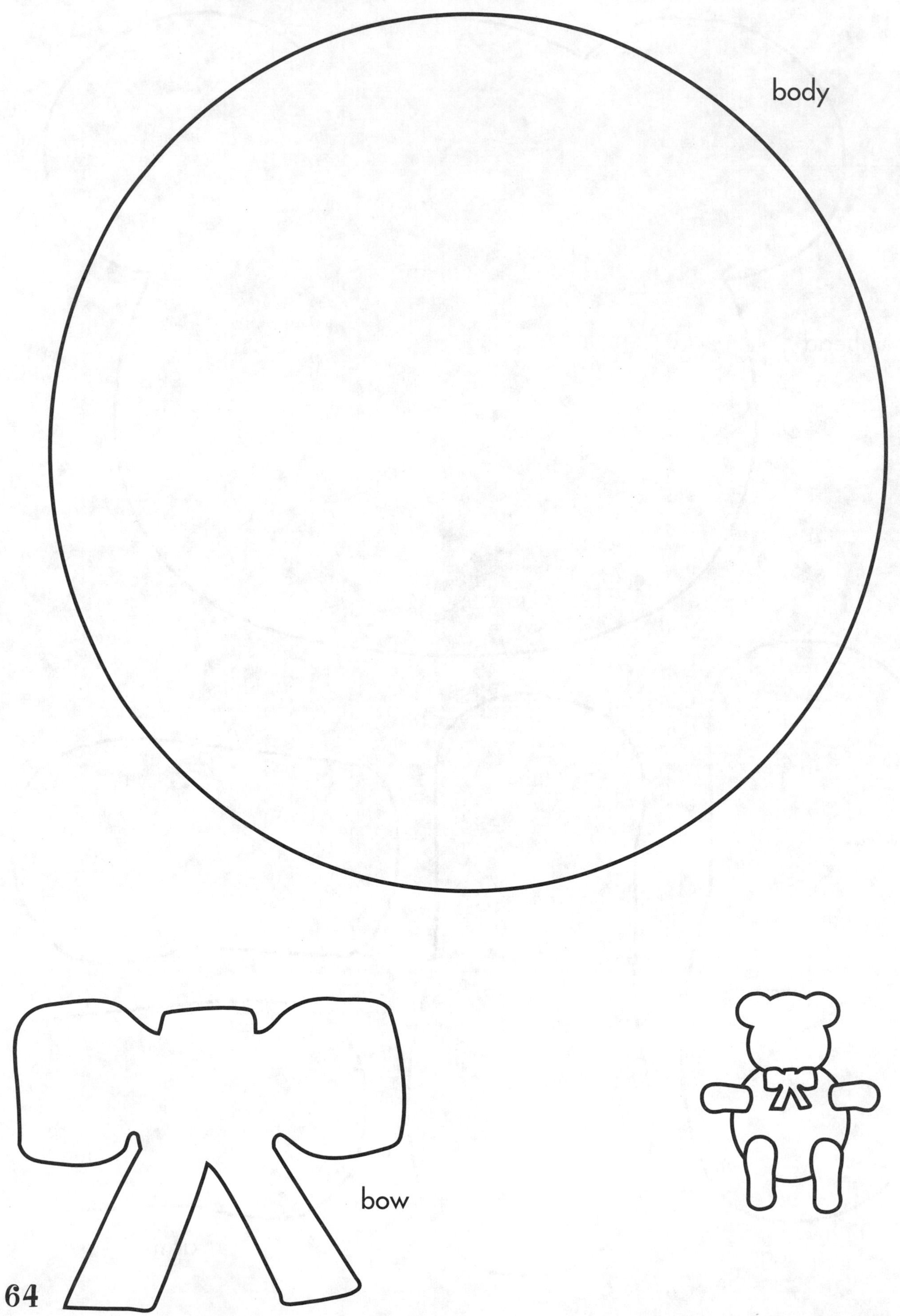
body
bow

Leaf, Leaf, Leaf

Six Little Snowflakes

bird
dog
rabbit
frog
duck

Pocket Charts for Making Things

The activities in this section can benefit children in a number of ways. They give students practice in reading and following directions. Activities that involve cutting with scissors, tracing, drawing outlines with templates, copying designs, and folding paper help children develop fine motor skills and eye-hand coordination. Activities that include matching shapes, finding missing parts, and working with designs are important for perceptual development which in turn contributes to better academic performance, particularly in reading.

A Jack-in-the-Box

PURPOSE

To match geometric shapes, do a simple paper folding activity, trace templates, and complete a picture.

MATERIALS

- 34" x 42" pocket chart
- 7 sentence strips
- Jack-in-the-box templates (page 73)
- construction paper in various colors, approximately 1 12" x 18" piece per child in class
- scissors
- glue
- permanent marker
- crayons or markers

SETUP

1 Write directions rebus style on sentence strips. Use a different color strip for each sentence. Place directions in the chart.

POCKET CHART WORDS

A Jack-in-the-Box

1. Trace and cut a square.
2. Trace and cut a rectangle. Fold your rectangle.
3. Trace and cut a large and small triangle.
4. Trace and cut a circle. Draw a face.
5. Trace and cut two zig-zags.
6. Glue your Jack-in-the-box together.

2 Model the activity by tracing and cutting shapes from templates as described in the directions.

3 Assemble the Jack-in-the-box and place it in the chart.

4 Before children start to make their own Jack-in-the boxes, discuss the name of each shape and how it will be used to make the Jack-in-the-box. (I.e., the circle is for the face; the small triangle is the hat; we are folding the rectangle so that it looks like it's popping, and so on.)

5 You may want to set this up as an independent center, or have children work with you in small groups.

Variations

1 Cut extra shapes from tagboard and use for a shape sorting activity.

2 Glue each completed Jack-in-the-box onto a piece of 12" x 18" construction paper. Make a class big book or bulletin board display. Write this sentence start on a sentence strip and have each child dictate a completion: A Jack-in-the-box . . .

Replies will vary: "A Jack-in-the-box is funny." "A Jack-in-the-box makes me laugh." "A Jack-in-the-box pops when you wind it."

Literature Integration

Alexander the Wind-Up Mouse by Leo Lionni. Random House, 1989.

Rake the Leaves

PURPOSE

To trace lines, use templates and color cues, follow directions, and complete a picture.

MATERIALS

- 34" x 42" pocket chart
- 3 white sentence strips, 2 blue sentence strips, and 1 each in green, orange, pink, yellow, purple, red, and brown
- rake and leaf templates (pages 65 and 74–75)
- tagboard
- red, yellow, green, blue, purple, brown, orange Tru-Ray construction paper

(Each child will need a piece of each color sized according to each template.)

- glue
- scissors
- colored markers (permanent if possible)

POCKET CHART WORDS

Rake the Leaves

1. Trace and cut a yellow rake.
2. Trace and cut a blue handle. Glue it to the rake.
3. Trace and cut one green leaf, one orange leaf, one purple leaf, one red leaf, one brown leaf.
4. Glue the five leaves to the rake.

SETUP

1 Write pocket chart instructions rebus style as shown in the photo. Use the different color sentence strips and/or markers to correspond to leaf colors.

2 Make and mark templates as shown.

3 Make a complete rake.

4 Place directions and templates in the chart. Attach a completed rake to chart with easel clip or butterfly clip.

5 Place construction paper needed near chart.

6 Read directions with children and demonstrate how to put the rake together. This can be an independent center activity or a small group activity with assistance depending on the age of the children.

Variations

1 Coordinate this activity with the "Leaf, leaf, leaf" poem on page 58.

2 Have children write color words on the rakes.

3 Children may want to write a color poem and glue it to the rake. Try brainstorming words to fit this pattern:

Fall is as red as. . .
Fall is as green as. . .
Fall is as purple as. . .
Fall is as orange as. . .
Fall is as brown as. . .

A finished poem may look like this:

Fall is as red as an apple.
Fall is as green as the grass.
Fall is as purple as a grape.
Fall is as orange as a pumpkin.
Fall is as brown as a chocolate bar.

4 These rakes make an excellent bulletin board display.

Literature Integrations

A Tree is Nice by Janice May Udry. Harper Trophy, 1956, 1987.

Why Do Leaves Change Color? by Betsy Maestro. Harper Trophy, 1994.

Teddy Bear

PURPOSE

To practice tracing templates, cutting, and putting pieces together correctly.

MATERIALS

- 34" x 42" pocket chart
- teddy bear templates (pages 63–64)
- brown construction paper
- tagboard for templates
- buttons and pom poms
- scissors
- glue
- paper fasteners
- permanent marker
- markers

POCKET CHART WORDS

Teddy Bear

1. Trace and cut the head.
2. Trace and cut the body.
3. Trace and cut two arms.
4. Trace and cut two legs.

Put your Teddy Bear together with fasteners. Draw a face.

SETUP

1. Using the templates, trace the teddy bear onto tagboard. Cut the teddy bear parts and fasten them together.
2. Write directions on sentence strips.
3. Place teddy bear, directions, and templates in chart.
4. Read directions with children demonstrating how the teddy bear goes together. Younger children may need help with the paper fasteners.

Variations

1. You may wish to coordinate this activity with the teddy bear poem on page 57.
2. These teddy bears make a wonderful display on a bulletin board or mural paper. Children can dictate a teddy bear rhyme to be written on a sentence strip and tacked over or under their bear.

Literature Integrations

Teddy Bear, Teddy Bear by Kathleen Hague. Scholastic, 1991.

Golden Bear by Ruth Young. Penguin, 1992.

If Eggs Could Talk

PURPOSE

To create a booklet.

MATERIALS

- 34" x 42" pocket chart
- 7 sentence strips
- egg, basket, and talk bubble templates (page 76)
- construction paper
- hole puncher
- ribbon

SETUP

1. Write pocket chart word directions on sentence strips.
2. Trace the templates and create a sample booklet.
3. Place directions, templates, and sample in chart.
4. Read children stories about eggs. Brainstorm a list of animals that hatch from eggs.
5. Read chart and demonstrate how to make pages and the cover for the booklet.
6. Place bubble pages nearby for those children who can write. Younger children can dictate words to be written on bubbles.

Variations

1. Coordinate this activity with "These eggs are talking" on page 44.
2. Work on this as a whole class, having each child contribute one page.
3. Have children do the activity in groups. Each group can work on a different animal group, such as land animals, water animals, and animals that fly.

POCKET CHART WORDS

If eggs could talk. . .

1. Trace, color, and cut eggs.
2. Glue just the flap of each egg onto a page.
3. Draw a scene around each egg.
4. Draw an animal inside the egg (under the egg flap).
5. Write a talk bubble. Glue it to the page.
6. Trace, cut, and color the basket cover.

Literature Integrations

Just Plain Fancy by Patricia Polacco. Bantam, 1990.

The Egg by Gallimard Jeunesse and Pascale de Bourgoing. Scholastic, 1992.

A Jack-in-the-Box

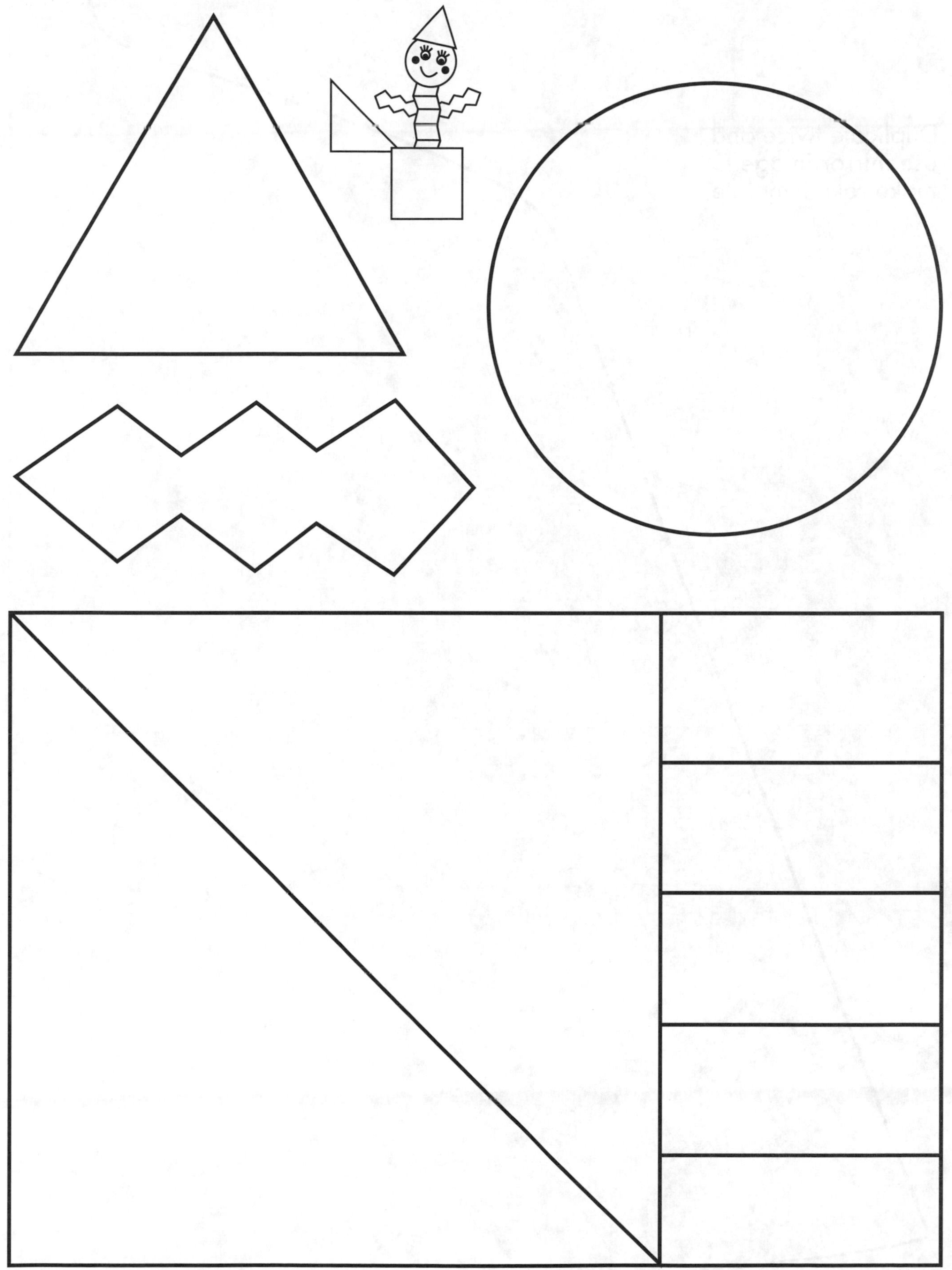

Duplicate twice and use mirror image to make rake template.

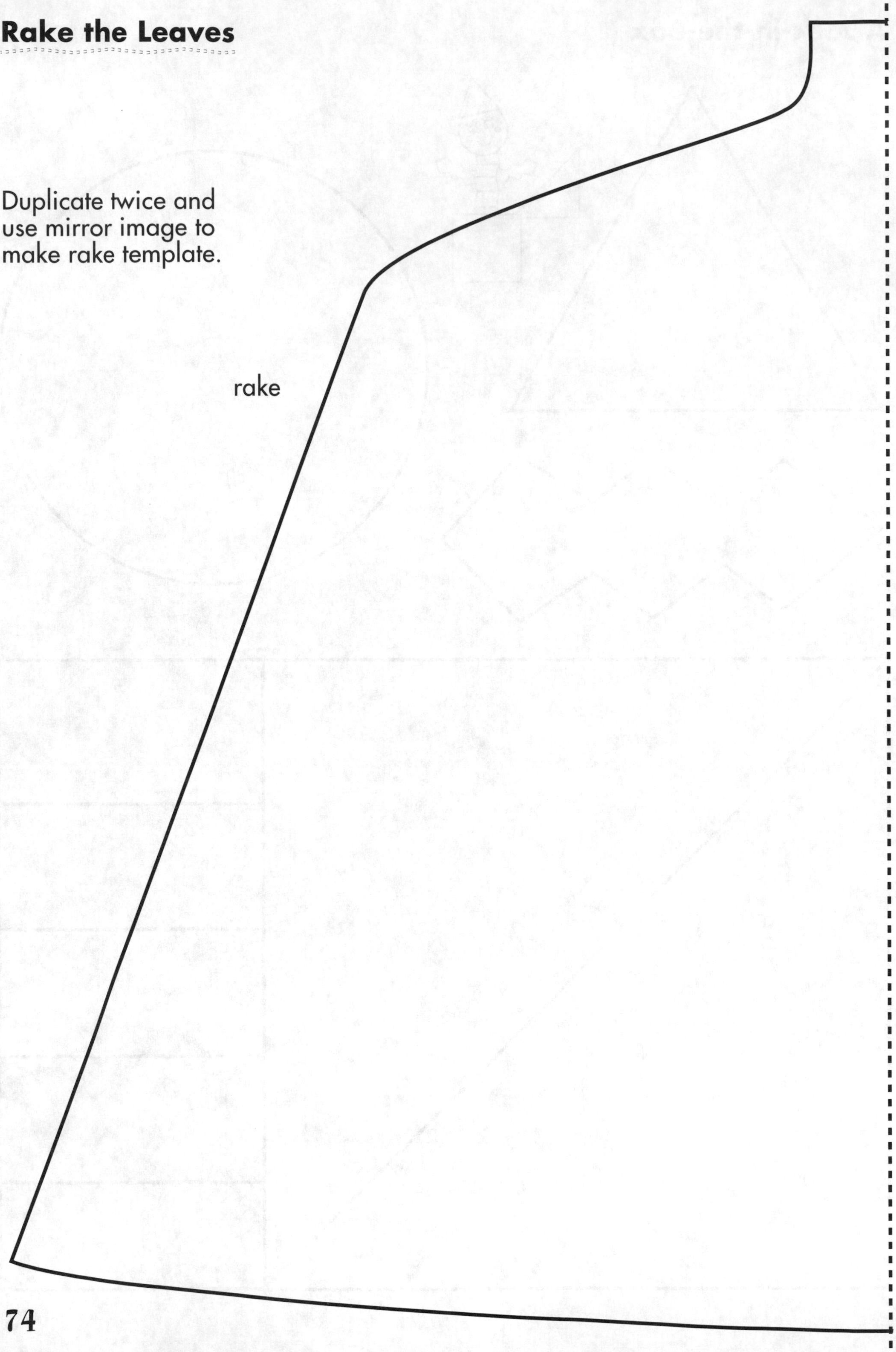

rake

Rake the Leaves

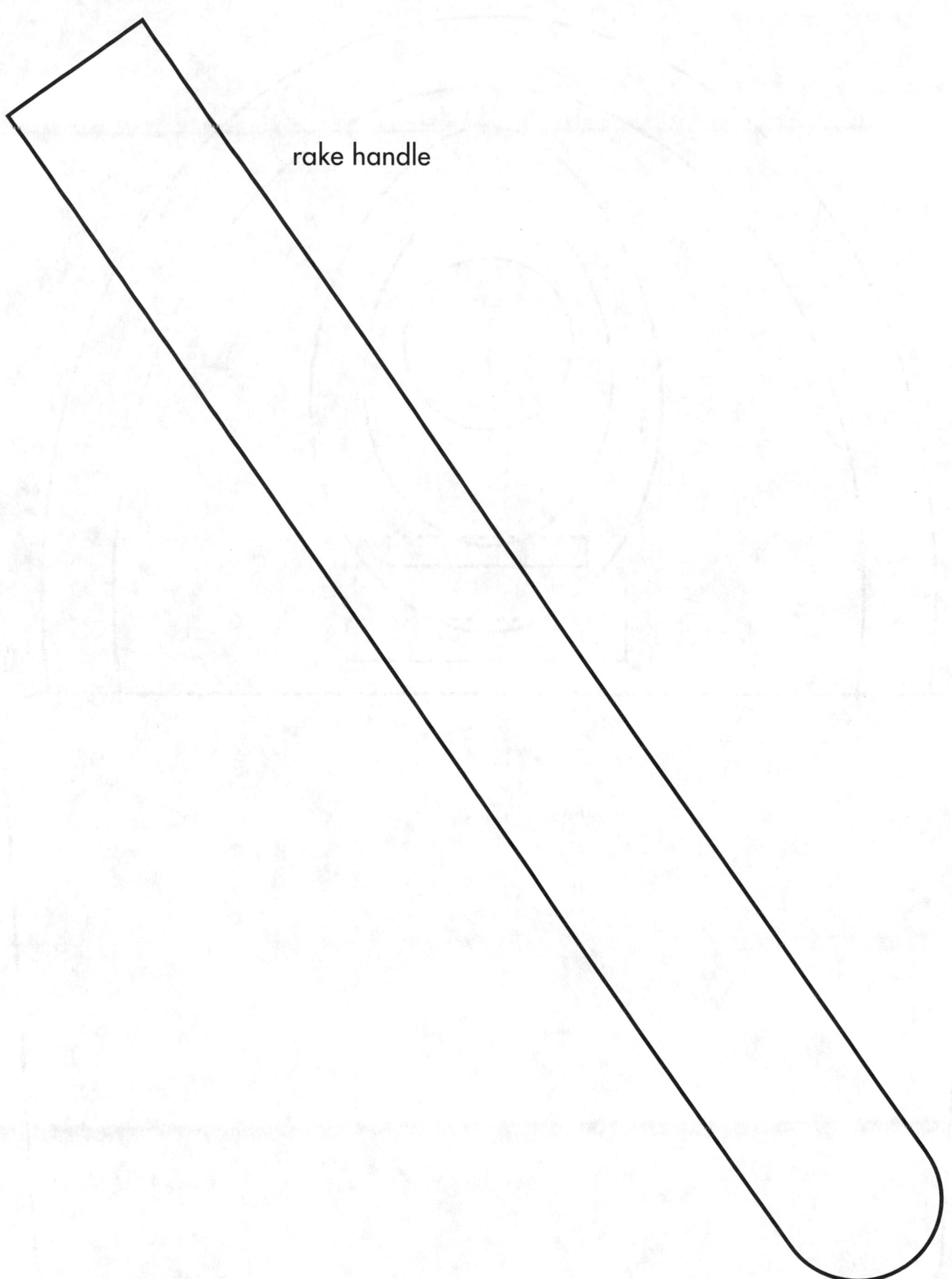

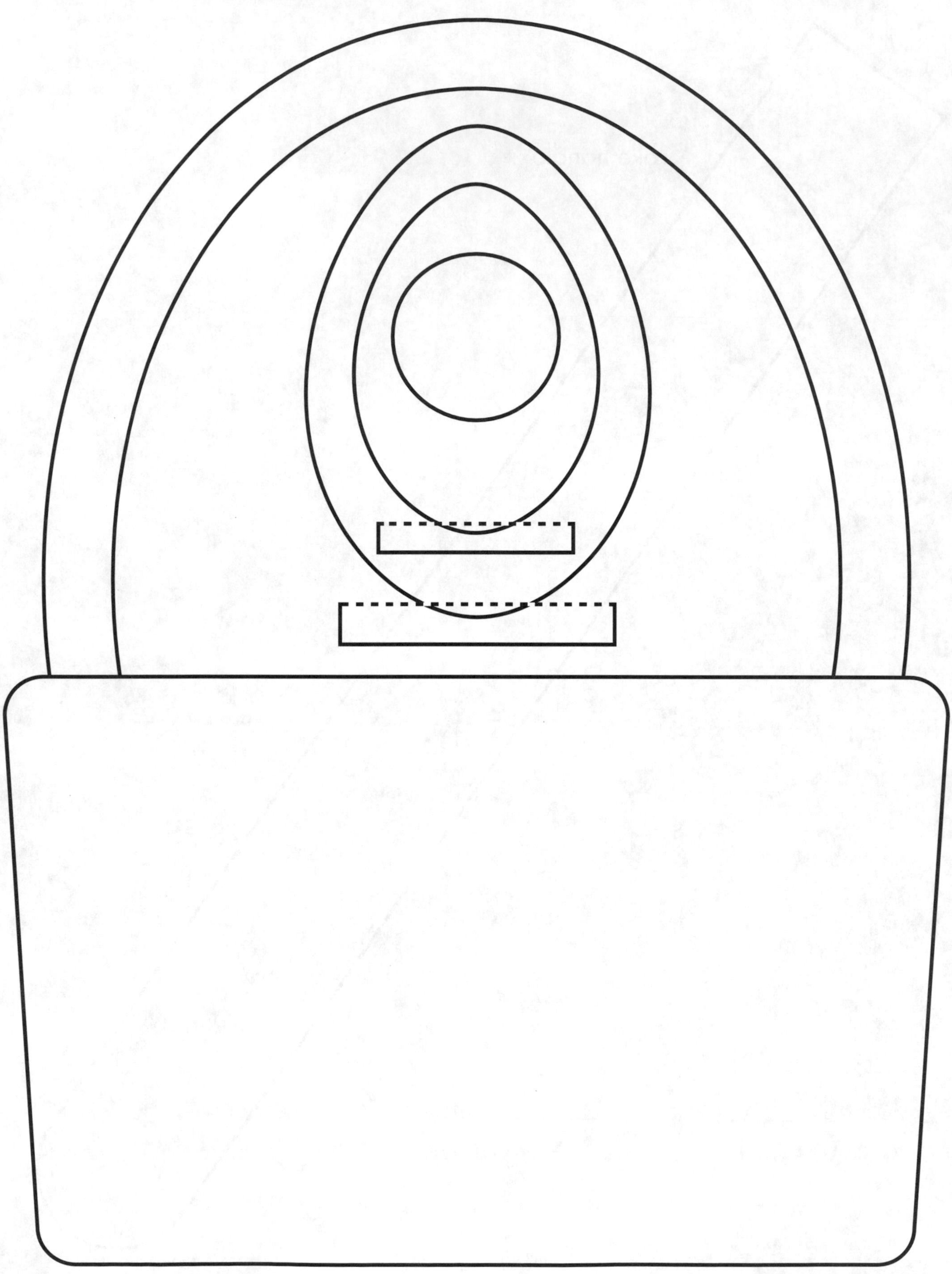

Pocket Charts to Count On

Mathematics is a symbolic language. As with reading, repetition will help children learn numbers and symbols. These pocket charts use concrete materials to build upon the mathematical concepts children are developing.

Ten Tens Trail Mix

PURPOSE

Children practice counting to ten and recognizing number words. Older children will recognize that they are counting by tens to one hundred.

MATERIALS

- 34" x 42" pocket chart
- 10 sentence strips of various colors
- permanent markers
- white 4-ply tag
- food templates (pages 84–86)
- colored markers or crayons
- chocolate chips, peanut butter chips, apple pieces, popcorn, small pretzels, banana chips, pumpkin seeds, walnuts, raisins, sunflower seeds
- zip-lock sandwich bags (1 for each child in your class)

You may want to assign each child a food and an amount of it to bring into school.

SETUP

1. Write directions on sentence strips of various colors; cut sentence strips to size as shown in the photo.
2. Trace, color, and cut food illustrations.
3. Place sentence strips in pocket chart (see photo).

POCKET CHART WORDS

Ten Tens Trail Mix

Count to ten then count again until you have ten tens in your zip-lock bag.

10 sunflower seeds

10 raisins

10 chocolate chips

10 pretzels

10 peanut butter chips

10 apple pieces

10 pieces of popcorn

10 banana chips

10 pumpkin seeds

10 walnuts

Zip your bag tight!

Shake and eat.

4. Place food illustrations in a zip-lock sandwich bag.

5. Set up real food in bowls with spoons buffet style so that children can walk by in turn to count the food into their bags. You may need a couple of buffet lines depending on the number of children in your class. The management technique you use will depend on the number of children and space available in your room.

6. Explain to your class that you are making a special snack. Read the pocket chart words with the children. Practice counting to 10.

7. Hold up your zip-lock bag with the tag illustrations of the food. Give children turns to match the illustrations and place these in the chart correctly next to the corresponding words.

8. Repeat the directions and practice counting to ten. Then explain how each child will fill their bag while counting to ten ten times.

Variations

1. For younger children change the number from 10 to numbers 1-10. Children can count a different amount of each food item into their bags.

2. Use different kinds of finger foods.

3. Have a picnic in a park or on your playground with the trail mix.

ESL Variation

Use this chart to practice counting to 10. It is also an opportunity for children to learn vocabulary especially words for describing food, e.g., crunchy nuts, salty pretzels, squishy sweet raisins.

Literature Integrations

One Smiling Grandma by Ann Marie Linden. Penguin, 1992.

One to One Hundred by Teri Sloat. Dutton, 1991.

Count-A-Saurus by Nancy Blumenthal. Macmillan, 1989.

One Hundred is a Family by Pam Munoz Ryan. Hyperion Books for Young Children, 1994.

The Farmyard

PURPOSE

To practice counting and to match numerals to the correct number of objects.

MATERIALS

- 42" x 58" pocket chart
- 10 sentence strips, 2 each of 5 colors
- animal templates (pages 87–88)
- black, orange, white, pink, gray, brown, yellow construction paper or tagboard
- black permanent marker
- scissors

SETUP

1. Write each line of the poem on a sentence strip. Use the same color sentence strip for each couplet.
2. Trace and cut animals.
3. Place poem and animals in chart.
4. Read poem with children counting the groups of animals after reading each line.

> **POCKET CHART WORDS**
>
> **"The Farmyard"**
> (poem by A. A. Atwood)
>
> One black horse standing by a gate.
> Two plump cats eating from a plate.
> Three big goats kicking up their heels.
> Four pink pigs full of grunts and squeals.
> Five white cows coming slowly home.
> Six small chicks starting off to roam.
> Seven fine doves perched upon a shed.
> Eight gray geese eager to be fed.
> Nine young lambs full of frisky fun.
> Ten brown bees buzzing in the sun.

5. Reread poem having individual children come up to the chart to count the animals.

Variations

1. Place only the poem in chart and place the animals in chart as you read.
2. Work on ordinal numbers with children by having them point to each of the animals in the row and name first, second, third, and so forth.
3. Make a class big book of the poem. Write words on sentence strips. Glue to pieces of paper. Have children draw animals. Cut animals and glue to pages.

Literature Integrations

Old MacDonald Had a Farm illustrated by Rick Brown. Penguin, 1993.

The Farmyard Cat by Christine Anello. Ashton Scholastic, 1987.

When Cows Come Home by Chris Demarest. Boyds Mills Press, 1994.

Good Morning Chick by Mirra Ginsburg. William Morrow, 1980.

The Day Jimmy's Boa Ate the Wash by Trinka Hakes Noble. E.P. Dutton, 1980.

POCKET CHART WORDS

See the pretty flowers, We planted near the door.

A little boy picked one, And now there are four.

Four pretty flowers, For everyone to see.

The dog stepped on one of them, And now there are three.

Three pretty flowers, Yellow, pink, and blue.

The newsboy threw the paper, And now there are two.

Two pretty flowers, Sitting in the sun.

A caterpillar chewed the stems, And now there is one.

One little flower, With a smiling face.

I picked a pretty flower, And put it in a vase.

Five Pretty Flowers

PURPOSE

To countdown and to teach the concept of subtraction.

MATERIALS

- 10 green, 2 pink, 2 blue, 2 yellow, 2 orange, and 2 white sentence strips
- flower templates (page 89)
- crayons
- tagboard
- glue
- scissors
- black permanent marker

SETUP

1. Write the poem on sentence strips using green for the countdown phrases and different colors for each of the couplets.
2. Copy flowers. Glue to tagboard, color them, and then cut them out.
3. Place poem and flowers in pocket chart.
4. Read poem with children moving flowers between the lines to demonstrate the subtraction process.

Variations

1. Once the poem is read several times, children can act out poem pretending to be the flowers.
2. Give each child a copy of the template page and have them color and number the five flowers.
3. Make extra sets of flowers for individual children to use to work on subtraction.

ESL Variation

Focus on the action words, e.g., *stepped, picked, chewed, threw.*

Have children demonstrate actions. Ask "wh" questions:

Who picked a flower?

Who threw the paper?

What stepped on a flower?

What chewed a flower?

Where is the last flower?

What colors are the flowers?

Literature Integrations

Ten, Nine, Eight by Molly Bang. Penguin, 1985.

One Smiling Grandma A Caribbean Counting Book by Ann Marie Linden. Penguin, 1992.

Five Little Mice

PURPOSE

To practice the concept of serial order and relationships.

MATERIALS

- 8 orange and 6 green sentence strips
- mouse and food templates (page 90)
- permanent marker
- scissors
- glue
- tagboard

SETUP

1 Write the narration words of the poem on orange sentence strips. Write the "mouse talk" on green sentence strips. For older children you can begin to develop an awareness of quotation marks by noting that what the mice say

POCKET CHART WORDS

Five little mice hungry as can be went to the kitchen to see what they could see.

The first mouse found a cookie crumb. Ate it and said,

"Yum! Yum! Yum!"

The second mouse happily found some bread.

"That looks good to me!" he said.

The third mouse said, "What a break!

I just found the birthday cake!"

The fourth mouse seeing a big piece of cheese said,

"I'll eat this before anyone sees!"

Then the fifth mouse yelled,

"We'd better scat! Here comes that big yellow cat!"

is written on a different color strip.

2 Copy the mice (you'll need a total of five mice). Copy the food. Color, glue onto tagboard, and cut.

3 Place poem, mice, and food in pocket chart.

4 Count the mice. Read the poem with children.

5 Have children point to the first, second, third, fourth, and fifth mouse.

6 To sequence the events, ask children to try to remember what each mouse did.

7 Remove mice and food from the chart and give to individual children. Reread the poem. Have children replace mice and food as the line of the poem is read.

Variation

Have children pretend to be the mice and act out the poem.

Literature Integrations

Two Hungry Mice by Alan Baker. Penguin, 1990.

The Little Mouse, The Red Ripe Strawberry, and The Big Hungry Bear by Don and Audrey Wood. Child's Play, 1984.

A Busy Year by Leo Lionni. Alfred A. Knopf, 1992.

Ten Gray Squirrels

PURPOSE

To practice subtracting from ten by twos.

MATERIALS

- 5 white, 2 green, 2 yellow, 2 orange, and 2 pink sentence strips
- squirrel templates (page 100)
- gray tagboard
- scissors
- black permanent marker

SETUP

1 Write "The first one said," "The second one said," and so forth on five white sentence strips. Write each of the rhyming couplets on a different color sentence strip.

POCKET CHART WORDS

Ten gray squirrels sat near a tree.
The first two said, "Look at what we see!"
The next two said, "Children having fun!"
Then two said, "We should really run!"
Two more said, "Let's hide in the shade."
The last two said, "Well, we're not
afraid!"
But away they did run.
And then there were none.

2 Trace ten squirrels on gray tagboard and cut.

3 Place squirrels and poem in chart.

4 Read poem with children, pointing to and counting squirrels as you read.

5 Have five children come up and take two squirrels each out of the chart. Have the rest of the children count as they do this. Then reread the poem and have children replace squirrels. Count again. Repeat to allow more turns.

Variations

1 Have children pretend to be the squirrels and act out the poem.

2 Ask children to tell which words in the poem rhyme. Brainstorm a list of other words that rhyme with each couplet. Ask children if these new rhyming words would make sense in the poem.

ESL Variation

Focus on the words in the poem that tell the sequence of events, e.g., *first, next, then,* and *last.*

Literature Integrations

Squirrels by Brian Wildsmith. Scholastic, 1974.

Nuts to You by Lois Ehlert. Harcourt Brace Jovanovich, 1993.

Ten Tens Trail Mix

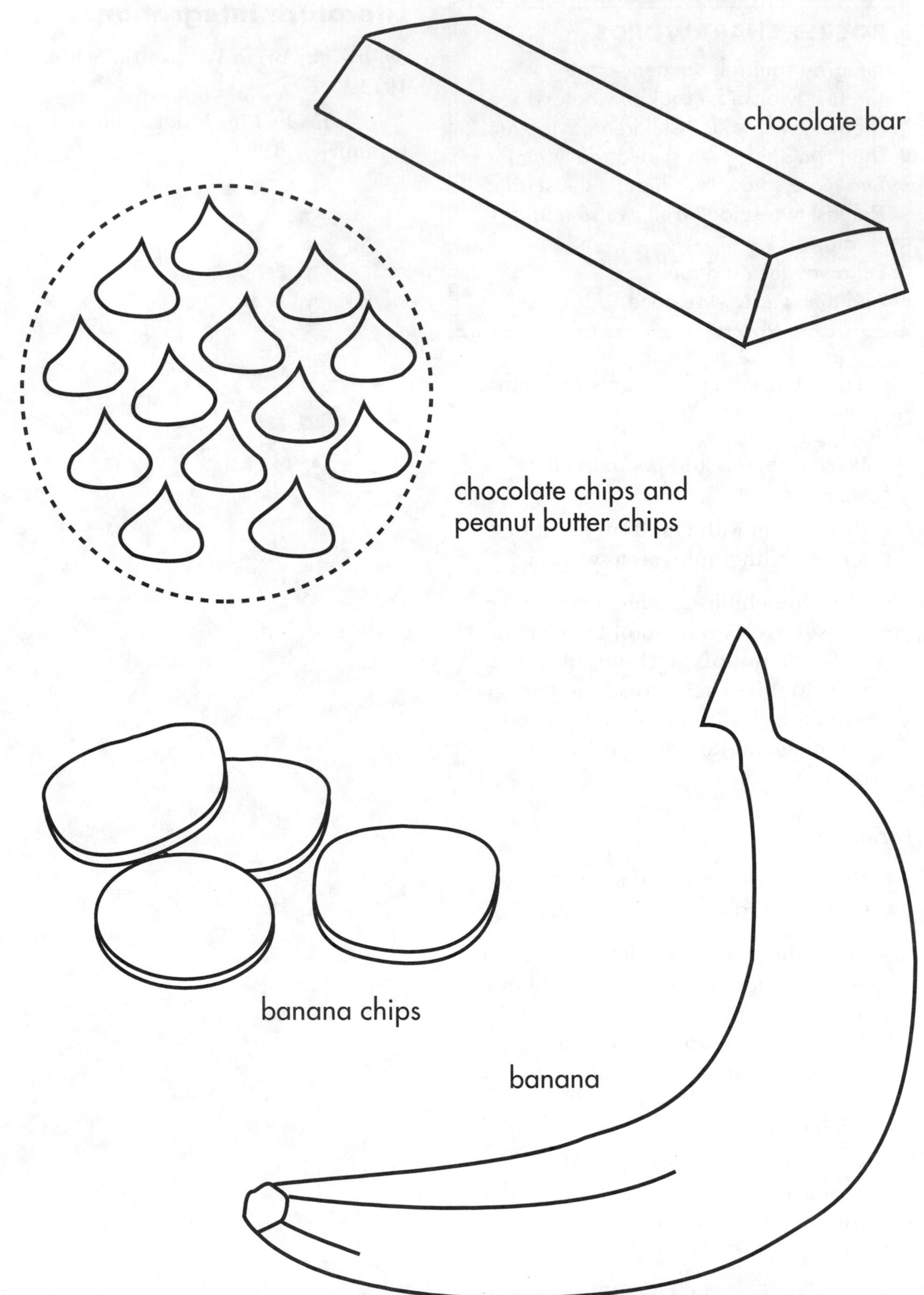

Ten Tens Trail Mix

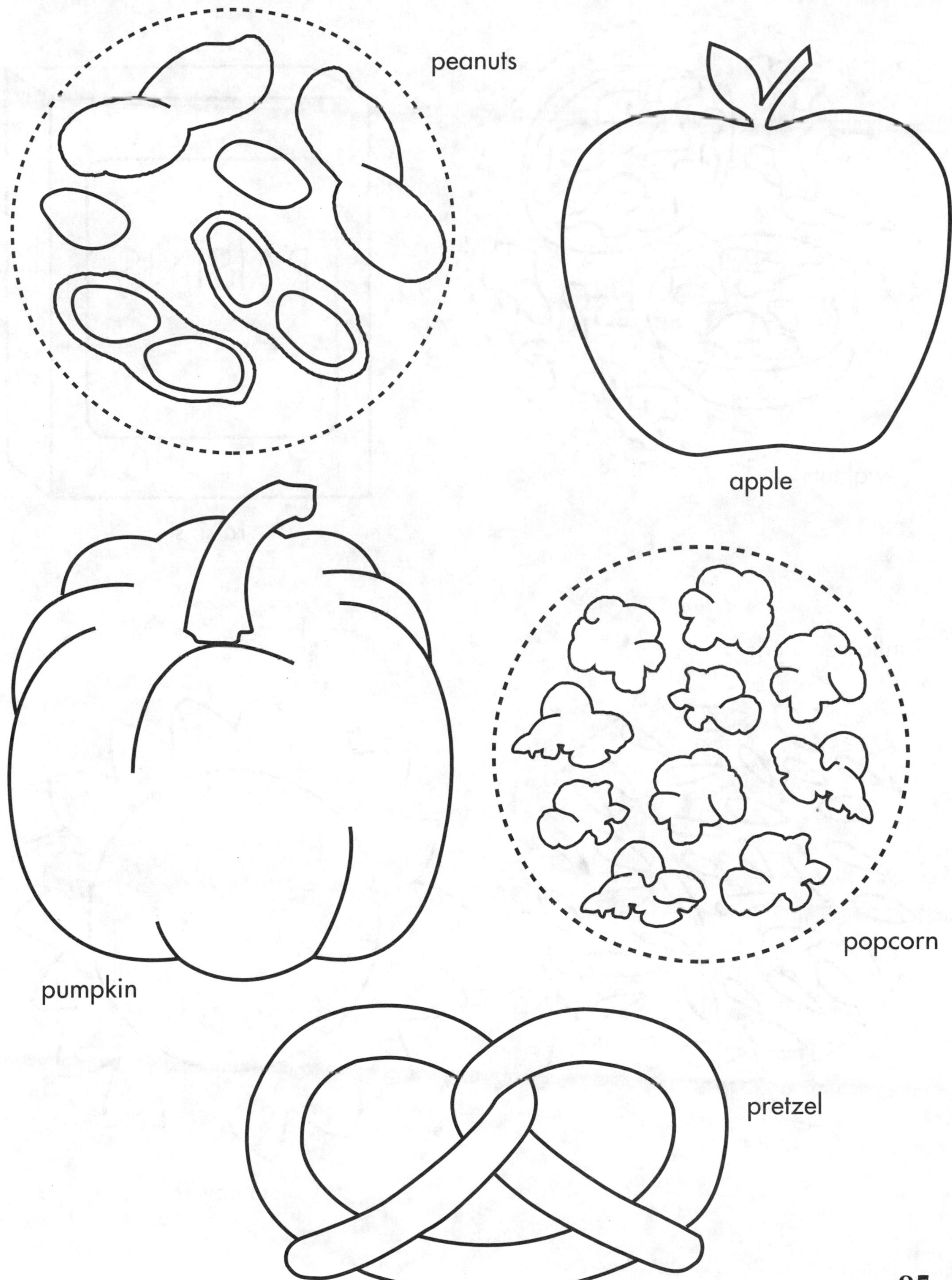

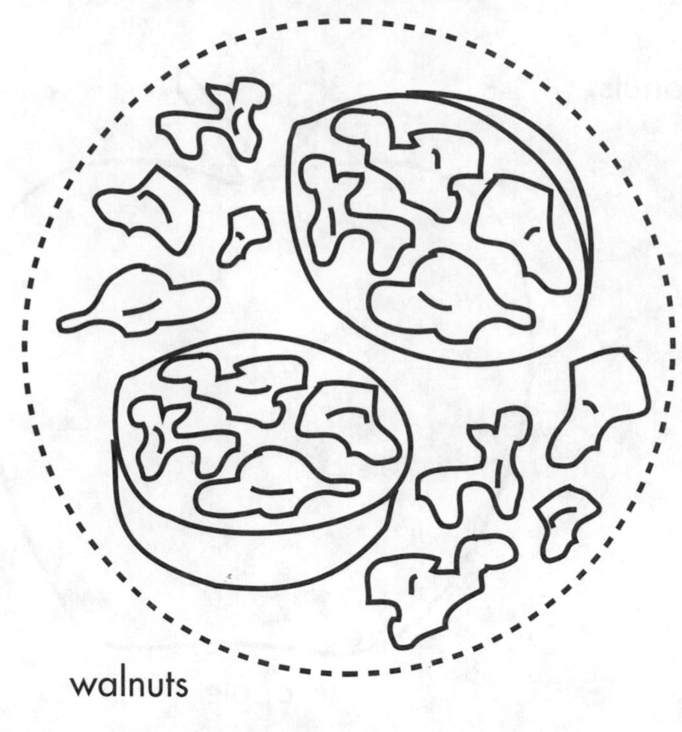

walnuts

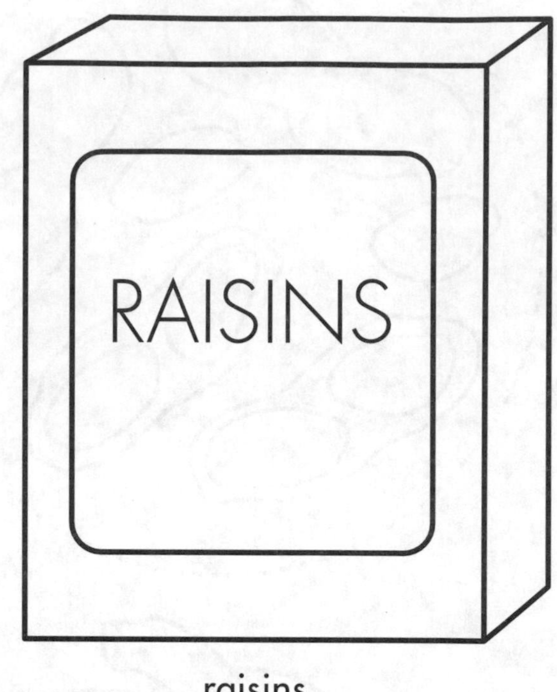

raisins

sunflower seeds

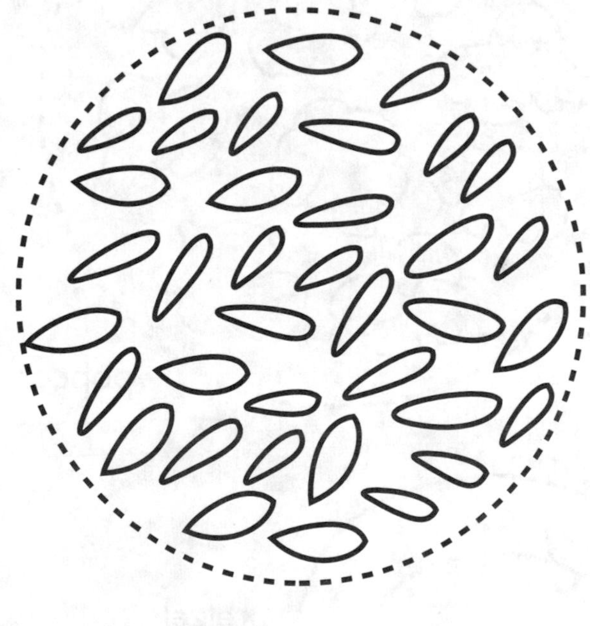

sunflower

The Farmyard

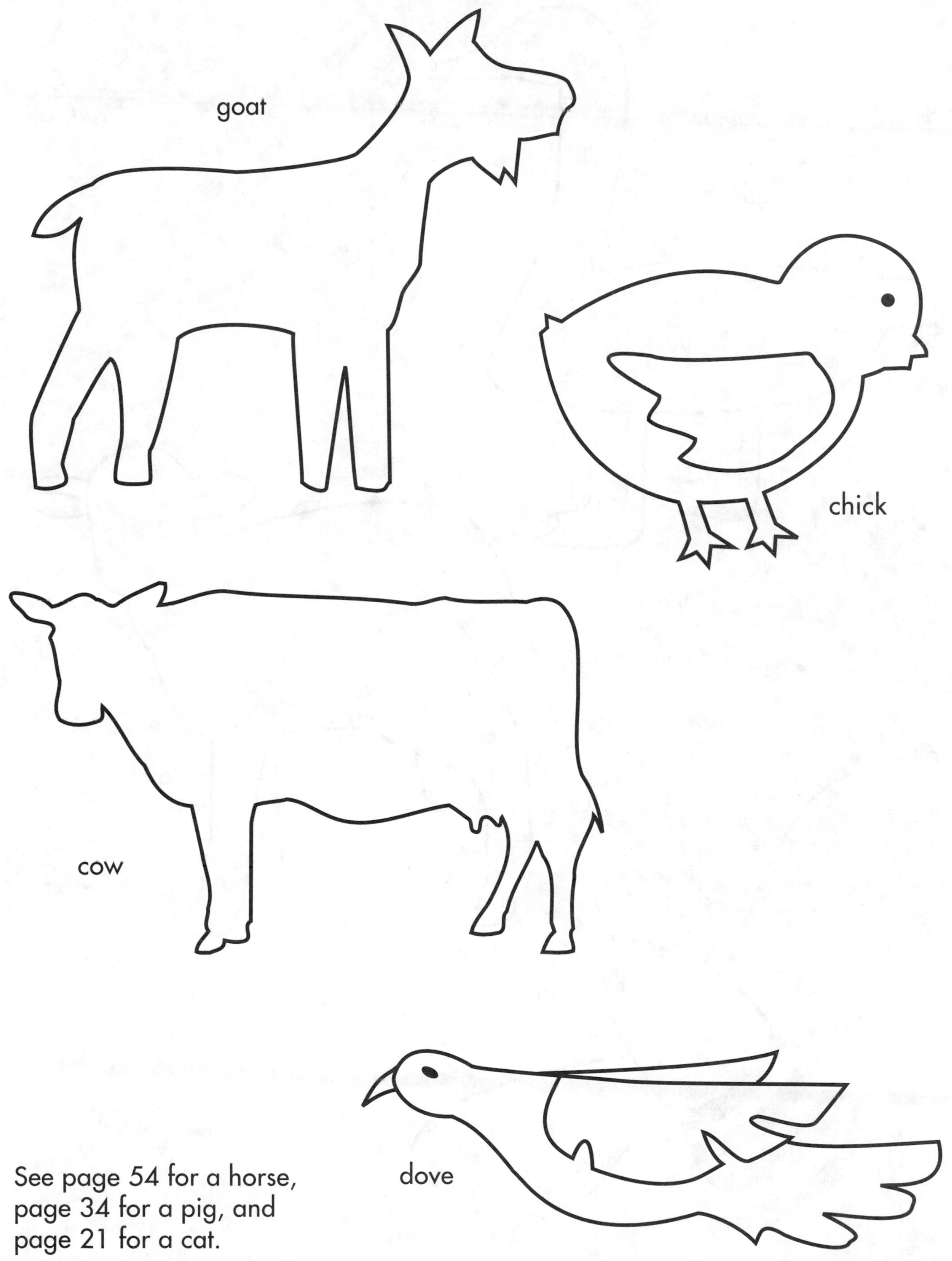

See page 54 for a horse, page 34 for a pig, and page 21 for a cat.

goose
lamb
bee

Five Little Mice

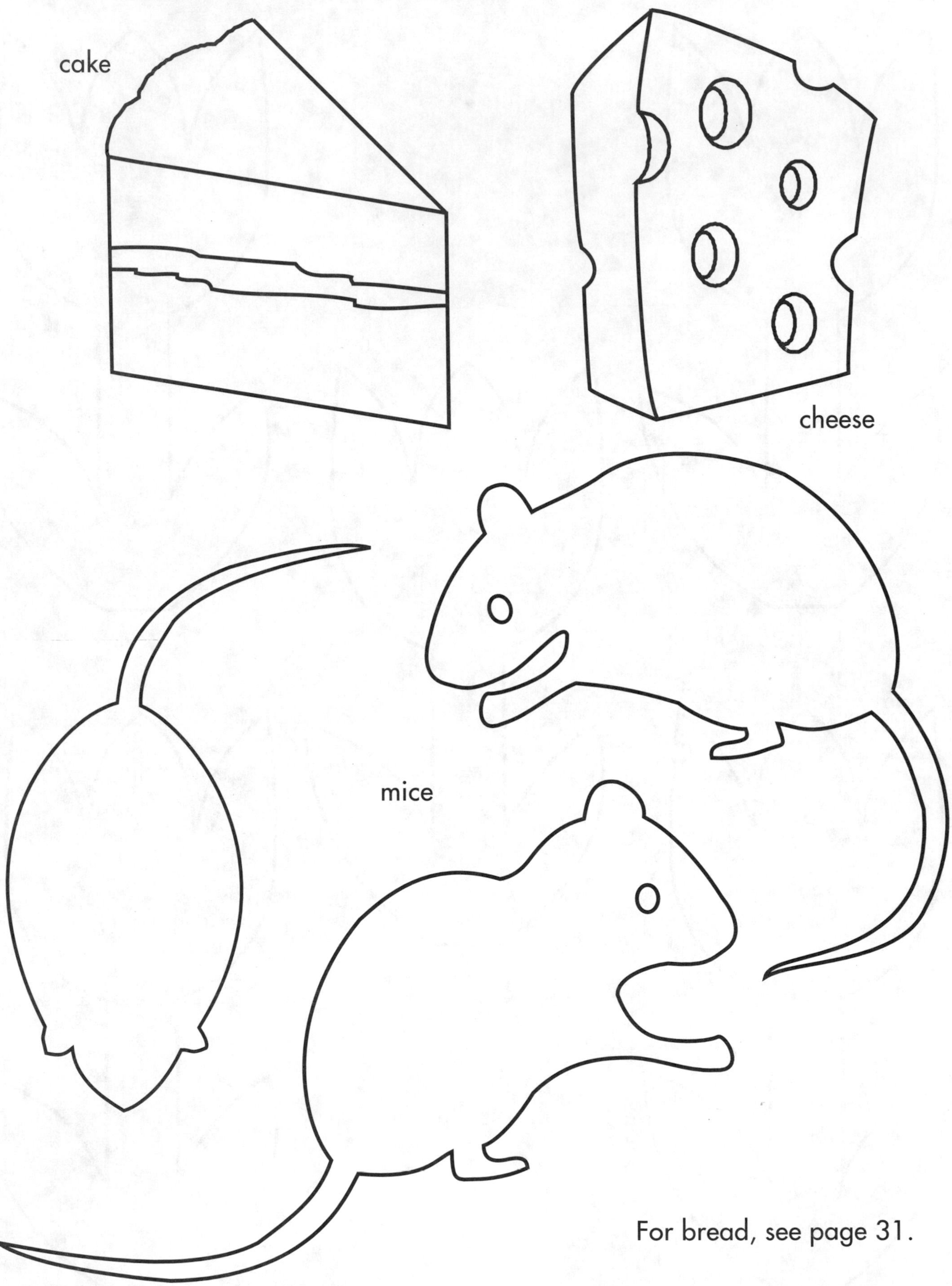

For bread, see page 31.

Predictable Pocket Charts

Children love "reading," reciting, recognizing, and repeating familiar words. The charts in this section give them practice predicting the words that come next. As they predict, they begin to develop their reading fluency.

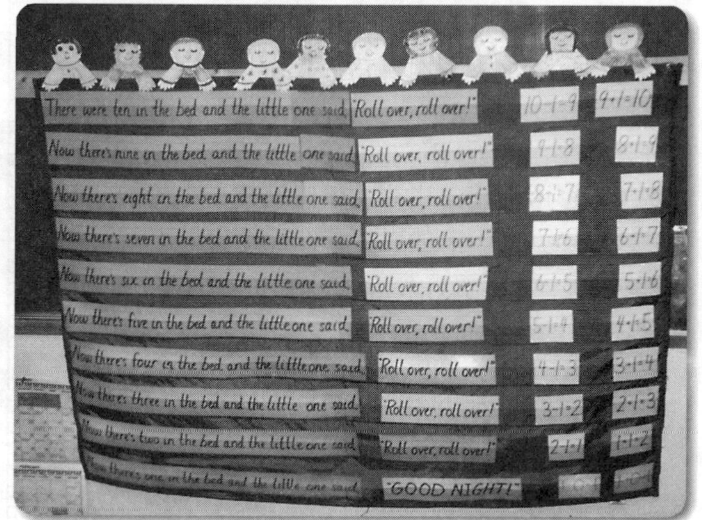

Ten in the Bed

PURPOSE

To encourage children to recite a predictable, repeated refrain and to recognize some sight words. To develop an understanding of subtraction.

MATERIALS

- 1 42" x 58" pocket chart or 2 34" x 42" pocket charts
- 10 orange sentence strips
- 3 yellow sentence strips (cut to size)
- 4 green sentence strips (cut to size)
- 3 blue sentence strips
- 4 white sentence strips (cut to size for "Good Night" and equations)
- children templates (page 98)
- 1 22" x 28" piece of 4-ply tag
- black permanent marker
- blue permanent marker
- multicultural crayons
- permanent markers in various colors

SETUP

1. Write "There were ten in the bed and the little one said," on orange strips; "Roll over, roll over!" on alternating green, yellow, and blue strips; and "GOOD NIGHT!" on a white strip. Use a black marker for the words so that children can also see a pattern in the chart. With more fluent readers you can point out that the parts in quotation marks are what is being said by the little one each time.

2. Write the equations in blue permanent marker on white strips. This will

separate the math from the poem. Place in the right hand side of the chart. Note: This can be omitted for younger children or if you choose not to include the math.

3 Trace, color, and cut 10 children to place on top of the chart as shown. Be sure to slit the arms along the dotted lines as indicated on the template. This will allow the arms to slip over the top of the pocket chart so it looks like the children are in the bed.

4 Place sentence strips in chart and arrange children along the top.

5 Read over the poem with the children once. Have them join in to chant the predictable "Roll over, roll over," as soon as they can.

6 Show the children how the "10 in the bed" can easily slip off the pocket chart. Then reread the poem and have the children join in. As you read, call children up to take turns slipping the children off the pocket chart one by one for the count down. Point to the subtraction equations as you and the children go through this process.

7 Then ask the children to tell you what would happen if one by one each of the children got back into the bed. Have the children return the "9 from the bed" back to the chart one by one and point out the addition equations. Then you can give the other children in your class a turn to repeat the activity.

Variations

1 Call ten children up to pretend to be the children in the bed. Have the class recite the poem as the children pretend to roll out of bed.

POCKET CHART WORDS

There were ten in the bed and the little one said, "Roll over, roll over!"

Now there's nine in the bed and the little one said, "Roll over, roll over!"

Now there's eight in the bed and the little one said, "Roll over, roll over!"

Now there's seven in the bed and the little one said, "Roll over, roll over!"

Now there's six in the bed and the little one said, "Roll over, roll over!"

Now there's five in the bed and the little one said, "Roll over, roll over!"

Now there's four in the bed and the little one said, "Roll over, roll over!"

Now there's three in the bed and the little one said, "Roll over, roll over!"

Now there's two in the bed and the little one said, "Roll over, roll over!"

Now there's one in the bed and the little one said, "GOOD NIGHT!"

10-1=9, 9+1=10, 9-1=8, 8+1=9, 8-1=7, 7+1=8, 7-1=6, 6+1=7, 6-1=5, 5+1=6, 5-1=4, 4+1=5, 4-1=3, 3+1=4, 3-1=2, 2+1=3, 2-1=1, 1+1=2, 1-0=1, 1+0=1

2 For younger children omit the addition and subtraction problems and just use the numbers 1-10 as a count down.

ESL Variations

1 Teach ordinal numbers by saying, "Touch (point to) the first, second third," and so forth.

2 Have one child or a pair of children get up in front of the class and give the command, "Roll over, roll over!"

3 As children memorize the rest of the song, have one child recite the verse:

"Now there's nine in the bed and the little one said," while the rest of the class says, "Roll over, roll over!"

4 For more advanced students, place the words *first, next, then, later,* and *finally* in the pocket chart. Have the children recite the poem using these signal words instead of the word *now.*

Literature Integrations

Roll Over! A Counting Song illustrated by Merle Peek. Houghton Mifflin, 1982.

There Were Ten in the Bed illustrated by Pam Adams. Child's Play, 1979.

Ten Out of Bed by Penny Dale. Candlewick Press, 1993.

The Right Number of Elephants by Jeff Sheppard. HarperCollins, 1990.

Concentration

PURPOSE

To recognize vocabulary and predict matching pairs.

MATERIALS

- 6 sentence strips
- copy of small pictures
- pink and yellow construction paper
- black and red permanent markers
- glue
- scissors

SETUP

1 Cut construction paper into 6"-pieces.

2 Write the vocabulary words on the yellow construction paper in black. You can write the beginning or ending sound in red to build phonics understanding. Cut out pictures that illustrate the words and glue them on the pink constrution paper.

3 Write the directions on different color sentence strips using a rebus style. Draw a yellow or pink rectangle around the color words.

POCKET CHART WORDS

Concentration

1. Turn over one pink picture card and one yellow word card.
2. See if the word and the picture match. Take the match cards out.
3. If not, turn one card back over. Try again.
4. Play until you match all the cards.

(The words will depend on the pictures you choose. You can use pictures from this book. Some suggestions are: *snow, fish, star, heart, egg.*)

4 Place yellow word strips and pink picture strips in pocket chart with reverse (blank) side showing.

5 Discuss what the word *concentration* means (thinking really hard).

6 Read the pocket chart directions with the children. Have children take turns turning over one of each color card as directed. Challenge children to remember where a particular card is or to predict which card is being turned.

7 Play the game as a class, in small groups, or in pairs. You may also want to set it up as a center. Change words as desired.

Variations

1 For younger players use picture cards and the first letter of the word.

2 For phonics reinforcement, write the first or last letter (or letters for blends and digraphs) of each word in a different color marker.

Literature Integrations

Look! Look! Look! by Tana Hoban. William Morrow & Co. 1988.

Each Peach Pear Plum by Janet Ahlberg and Allan Ahlberg. Viking Press. 1986.

It Was a Cloud

PURPOSE

Everyone loves to look up at the sky, see the clouds, and imagine what object each cloud looks like. This chart will help children use their imagination and practice predicting and recognizing repeated words in this chart.

MATERIALS

- 34" x 42" pocket chart
- 6 blue sentence strips
- 10 white sentence strips
- black marker
- 22" x 28" 4- to 6-ply white tag
- cloud templates (page 99)

SETUP

1 Write the words, "It looked like a . . ." 8 times and "It was a cloud in the sky," once on white sentence strips. Write

the words "But it wasn't a . . ." 8 times and "What does a cloud look like to you?" once on blue sentence strips.

2 Trace and cut the templates from white tagboard.

3 Hand the "cloud" shapes to children before you begin reading the chart.

4 Use the chart as a story telling prompt, by reading the sentence strips and placing them in the chart as you read. Very quickly the children will pick up on the word pattern and begin to repeat the refrains, "It looked like a . . . But it wasn't a . . ." You'll see them shaking their heads too.

5 As you read each sentence have the children come up and place the correct "cloud" shape in chart.

6 Read the story again giving other children turns to place "cloud" shapes in chart.

7 Have children answer the question, "What does a cloud look like to you?" Add their answers and corresponding words to chart.

Variations

1 Make a new chart. Have children answer the question, "What does a cloud look like to you?" Add their answers to the chart.

2 Go outside and look for cloud shapes. Then come back into the classroom and give children drawing paper to make their own clouds. Add these and corresponding words to chart.

3 Make a class big book of the cloud story. Children can cut their cloud shapes from white drawing paper or white felt. Then glue these onto blue paper. For best results, use 12" x 18" Tru-Ray construction paper. Write the words on sentence strips and glue these right to the pages.

POCKET CHART WORDS

It looked like a dragon. But it wasn't a dragon.
It looked like a cow. But it wasn't a cow.
It looked like a car. But it wasn't a car.
It looked like a dog. But it wasn't a dog.
It looked like a flower. But it wasn't a flower.
It looked like a fish. But it wasn't a fish.
It looked like a star. But it wasn't a star.
It looked like a snowman. But it wasn't a snowman.
It was a cloud in the sky.
What does a cloud look like to you?

Literature Integrations

It Looked Like Spilt Milk by Charles G. Shaw. HarperCollins, 1947.

Rain by Robert Kalan. Greenwillow Books, 1978.

Mouse's Marriage by Junko Morimoto. Penguin, 1986.

The Cloud Book by Tomie dePaola. Holiday House, 1975.

POCKET CHART WORDS

Whisky, frisky, Hippity-hop
Up he goes, To the treetop!
Whirly, twirly round and round
Down he scampers, To the ground.
Furly, curly What a tail.
Tall a feather, Broad as a sail.
Where is his supper? In the shell.
Snappity, crackity, Out it fell.

flop, mail, stop, nail, pail, found, sound, pop, pound, mound, well, tell, sell, bell, drop

Whisky Frisky

PURPOSE

To guess and predict the words that rhyme. Children get so excited by this poem, they can hardly sit still.

MATERIALS

- 34" x 42" pocket chart
- 8 green sentence strips
- 4-5 yellow sentence strips
- black marker, scissors
- tree and squirrel templates (pages 50–51 and 100)
- self-adhesive Velcro
- white, green, brown tagboard
- gray crayon

SETUP

(Note: If you also plan to make the "Who's in the tree?" chart (see page 40), this is the same tree. You can use it for both poems.)

1. Write the rhyming words like "hop, treetop, pop, stop," and so forth, on yellow sentence strips cut to size. This will increase students' awareness of the rhyming sounds. Write the main text on green sentence strips.
2. Trace and cut tree top, tree trunk, and squirrels from tagboard. Color squirrels as desired (gray, red, or brown).
3. Cut small pieces of Velcro for squirrels and tree. Be sure to attach the correct sides of Velcro to the tree, and the other side to the squirrel so the squirrels will stick.
4. Place all the words in chart as shown in the photo. You may also just place the poem words in the chart.
5. Set up tree by placing part of the base in chart and securing top with push pins. Have the squirrels handy to be placed on tree as you read.
6. Read poem with children placing squirrels on tree at appropriate intervals. For example, the squirrel with the nut at the bottom of the tree would be placed last.

7 As you read the poem, the correct rhyming words will be easily predicted by the children. When you have placed all the words in chart, have the children choose the correct rhyming words. Then you can also set up the chart with the words that rhyme placed together.

Variations

1 Before you read the poem, give several children the rhyming words. Have the class predict which word belongs in the poem. The child holding the correct word can place it in the chart as you read the poem.

2 Children enjoy repeating the poem, placing the squirrels, and trying different rhyming words. They'll laugh out loud as they try such nonsense as: "Furly, curly What a pail. Tall as a feather, Broad as a nail."

3 Place just the poem without the end rhymes in the chart. Read with your class. Then allow the children to generate words that rhyme. Write these on sentence strips and have children place them correctly in chart.

4 To emphasize the rhyme pattern, write each set of rhymes on different color sentence strips. Then sort the rhymes by sound and the color will be a self check. Children can work independently or with a partner.

Literature Integrations

Squirrels by Brian Wildsmith. Scholastic, 1974.

Nuts to You by Lois Ehlert. Harcourt Brace Jovanovich, 1993.

It Was a Cloud

Make Your Own Display Charts with Sentence Strips

Without using pocket charts, sentence strips alone can help you make some special displays.

Happy Birthday!

PURPOSE

To make a special birthday celebration chart.

MATERIALS

- 2 pieces of 22" x 28" 6-ply tag
- birthday cake, flowers, and candle templates (pages 106–107)
- 4 sentence strips for words plus one for each child in your class
- self-adhesive Velcro

SETUP

1. Make a copy of the cake templates and tape the two pieces together. Then trace and cut the cake.
2. Trace and cut flowers and candles. (The number of candles you will need depends on the age of the child whose

SENTENCE STRIP WORDS

Sing a happy birthday song.
Sing it sing it all day long.
Sing a happy birthday song
Just for ____________ .

(Names of children in your class)

birthday you are celebrating.)

3 Glue sentence strips, most of the flowers, and most of the candles onto cake as shown in photograph.

4 Glue three of the flowers just halfway on to create a ledge/holder for the name sentence strip.

5 Place a piece of Velcro on top of cake, large enough to hold the maximum number of candles you might need for your class.

6 On the day of a child's birthday, celebrate by placing the child's name and the correct number of candles on the cake. Finish by reciting the poem.

Literature Integrations

Mouse's Birthday by Jane Yolen. The Putnam & Grossett Group, 1993.

Happy Birthday Moon by Frank Asch. Prentice Hall, 1982.

See How I've Grown!

PURPOSE

To measure and compare height and growth throughout the school year.

MATERIALS

- 2 pieces of 22" x 28" 4- or 6-ply tag
- 4 to 6 sentence strips

> **SENTENCE STRIP WORDS**
>
> There's something about me
> That I'm knowing.
> There's something about me
> That isn't showing.
> I'm growing!
>
> 1 foot, 2 feet, 3 feet, 4 feet, 5 feet

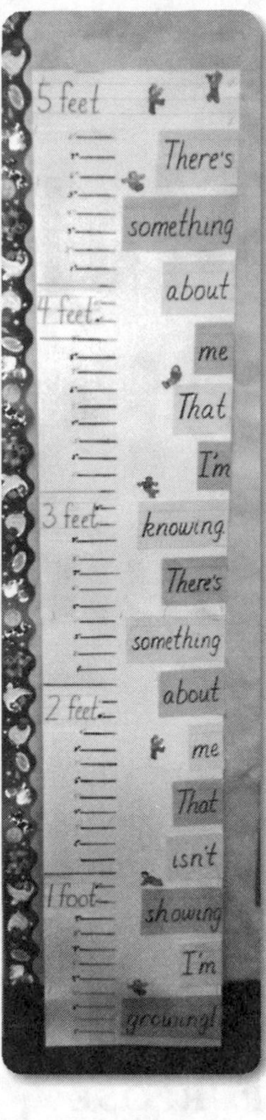

- ruler template (page 108)
- permanent marker
- scissors
- glue
- ruler copy

SETUP

1 Cut tag lengthwise. Lay out on floor to create five feet.

2 Measure and glue feet sentence strips onto the left side of the tagboard at one-foot intervals as shown in the photo.

3 Copy, cut, and glue ruler onto the left edge of the tagboard.

4 Write poem on different color strips for decorative purposes. Glue onto the right side of tagboard.

5 Find a wall space or the back of a door and hang by placing the two pieces of tagboard, edge to edge.

6 Give children turns to measure each other throughout the year. This is also a good way to start and end the year!

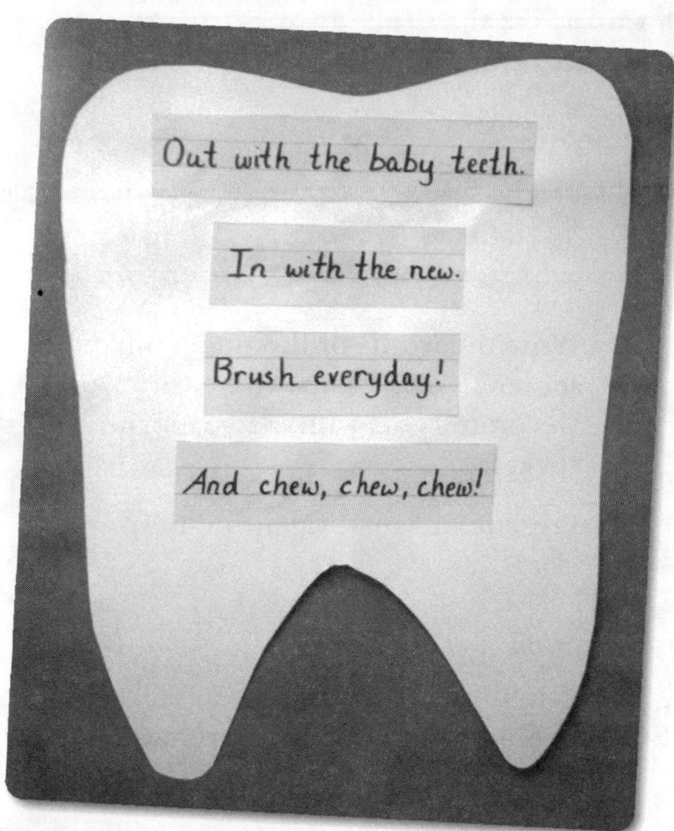

Tooth Poem

PURPOSE

To celebrate the loss of a tooth.

MATERIALS

- 22" x 28" white tag
- 3-4 sentence strips
- tooth template (page 109)
- permanent marker
- scissors
- glue

SETUP

1 Make copies of both parts of the tooth template. Tape together. Trace and cut tooth on white tagboard.

2 Write the words of the poem on sentence strips. Glue to tooth.

3 Read the poem with children to celebrate whenever somebody has lost a tooth. If you keep a tooth chart, you may wish to set this up near it.

SENTENCE STRIP WORDS

(poem by Valerie SchifferDanoff)

Out with the baby teeth
In with the new.
Brush everyday!
And chew, chew, chew!

Variations

1 Cut a small tooth for each child in your class. Write their names on it. Make a class display of teeth with the big poem tooth in the middle.

2 Give children a small sticker on their little tooth to keep track of teeth lost.

Literature Integrations

Little Rabbit's Loose Tooth by Lucy Bate. Scholastic, 1975.

Franklin and the Tooth Fairy by Paulette Bourgeois. Kids Can Press, 1996.

Happy Valentine's Day

PURPOSE

To celebrate Valentine's Day.

MATERIALS

- 22" x 28" 4-ply red tag
- heart template (page 110)
- 2 pink and 2 blue sentence strips
- permanent marker
- scissors
- glue
- lace trim
- stickers

SETUP

1 Copy the two parts of the heart template. Cut and tape the parts together. Then trace and cut from red tagboard.

SENTENCE STRIP WORDS

Valentines are red.
Valentines are blue.
I made this one,
Just for you!

2 Write the words of the poem on sentence strips. Glue to heart. Decorate heart with lace trim and stickers.

3 Present and read valentine to your class.

Variation

Have children draw or trace small hearts. Then color, cut, and glue them to the big heart. Older children can write short messages on the hearts.

Literature Integrations

Valentine's Day by Gail Gibbons. Holiday House, 1986.

Will You Be My Valentine by Steven Kroll. Holiday House, 1993.

Lunch Box

PURPOSE

To chant a poem that signals lunch time.

MATERIALS

- 22" x 28" 4-ply tag
- 5 sentence strips
- lunch box, sandwich, cookie, apple, carrot, and celery templates (pages 48 and 111)
- permanent marker
- scissors
- glue

SETUP

1. Make copies of both parts of the lunch box template. Tape them together and cut to shape.
2. Trace and cut lunch box from white tagboard.
3. Write poem on different color sentence strips. Glue to lunch box.
4. Copy sandwich, carrot, apple, celery, and cookie. Color, cut, and glue to lunch box.
5. Hang lunch box on the back of your classroom door.
6. Each time the children line up for lunch, say the poem several times. Soon they'll chant on their own, signaling lunch time!

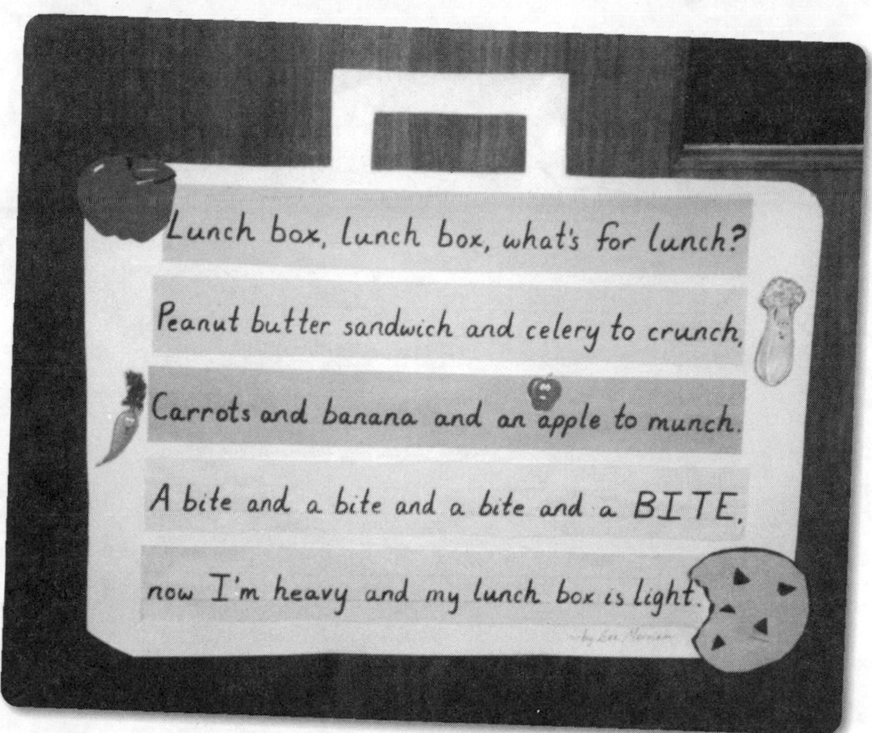

SENTENCE STRIP WORDS

(poem by Eve Merriam)

Lunch box, lunch box, what's for lunch?
Peanut butter sandwich and celery to crunch,
Carrots and banana and an apple to munch.
A bite and a bite and a bite and a BITE,
now I'm heavy and my lunch box is light.

Variations

1. Ask children about other foods they eat for lunch.
2. Substitute the new items for the ones in the poem, thereby, creating a new poem that the children can chant. Use corresponding pictures of food from magazines or newspapers to glue to the chart.

Literature Integrations

Lunch Boxes by Fred Ehrich. Penguin, 1993

Monster's Lunch Box by Marc Brown. Little Brown, 1995.

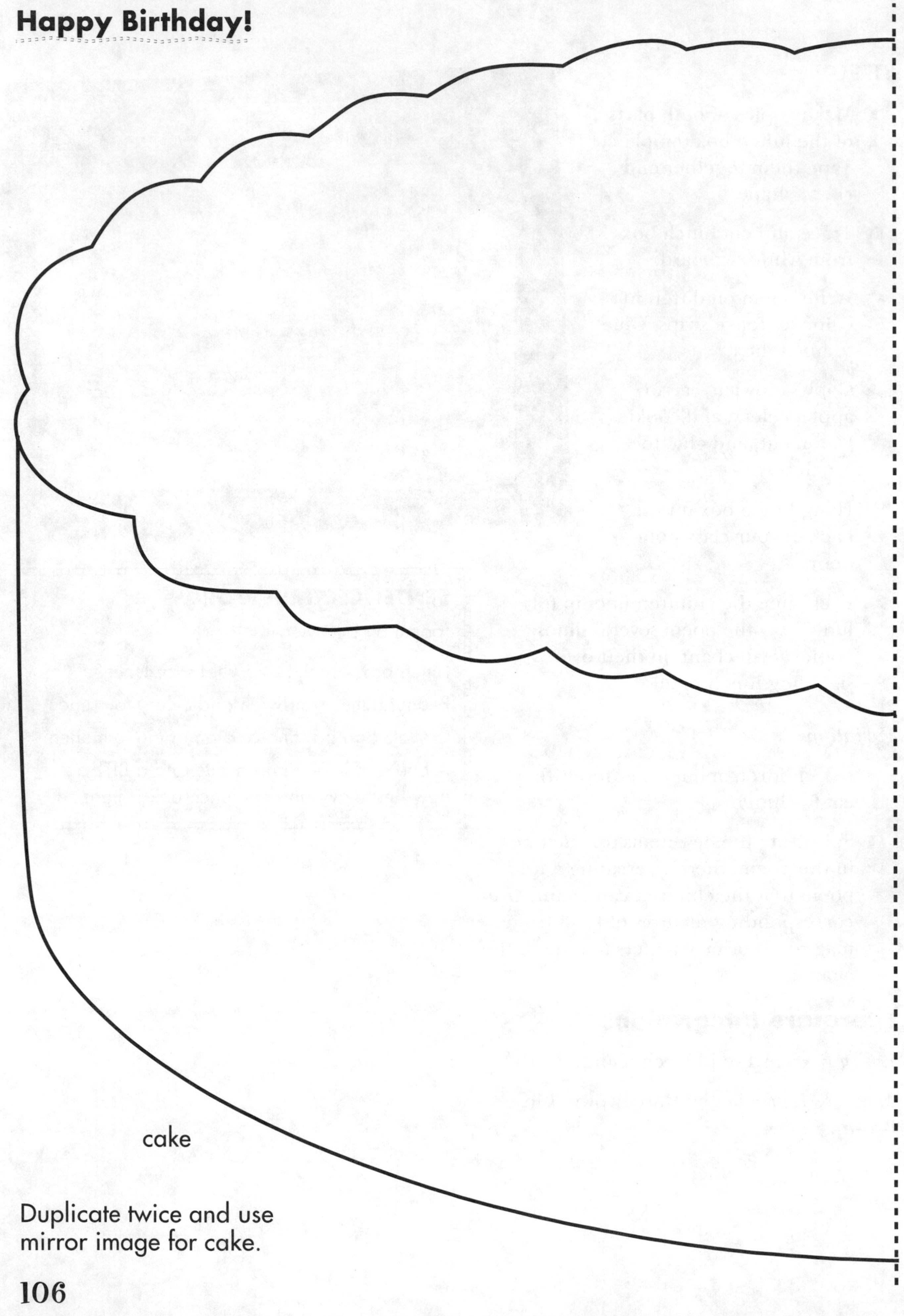

Duplicate twice and use mirror image for cake.

Happy Birthday!

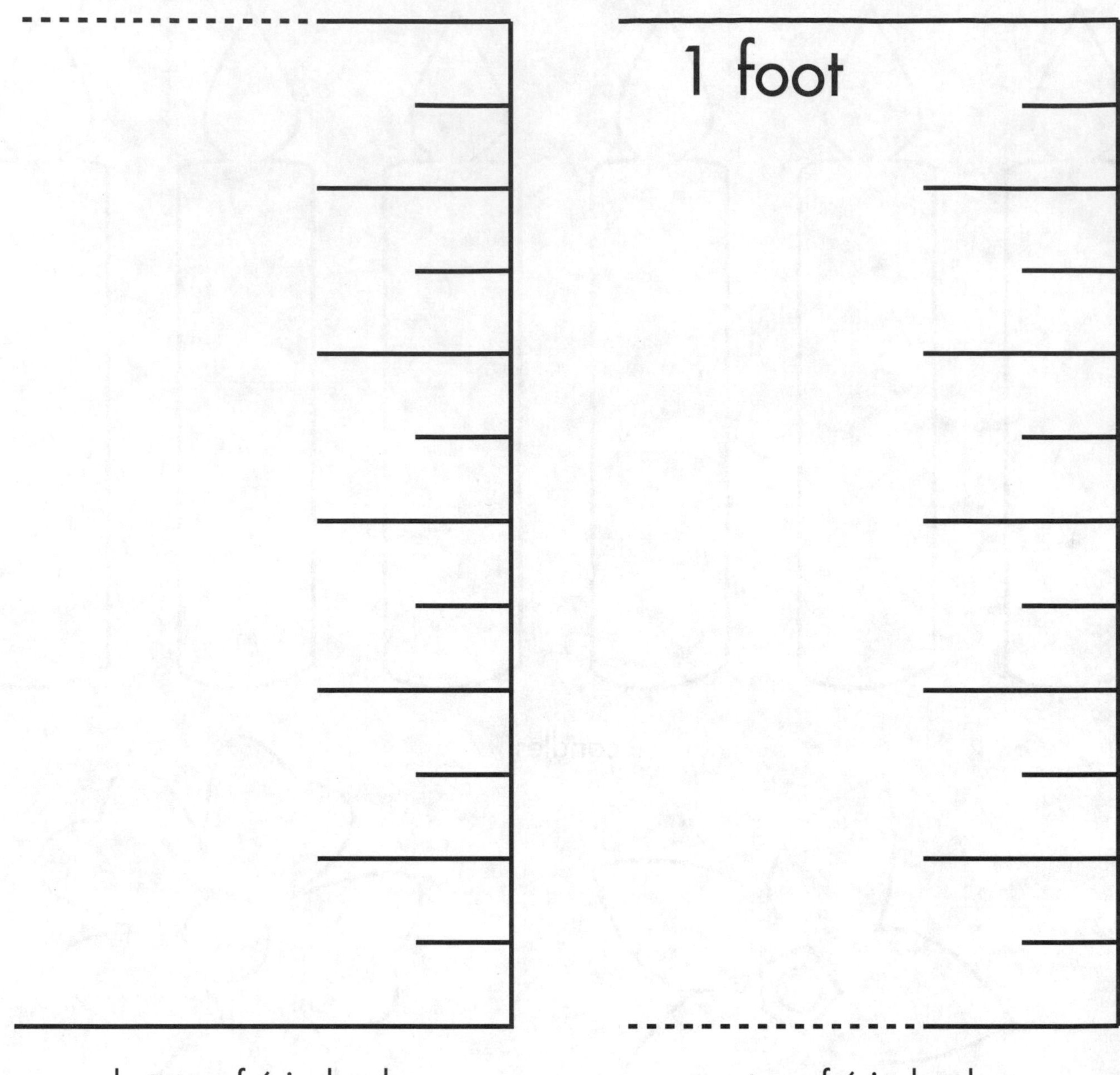

2 feet

3 feet

6 feet

4 feet

5 feet

Tooth Template

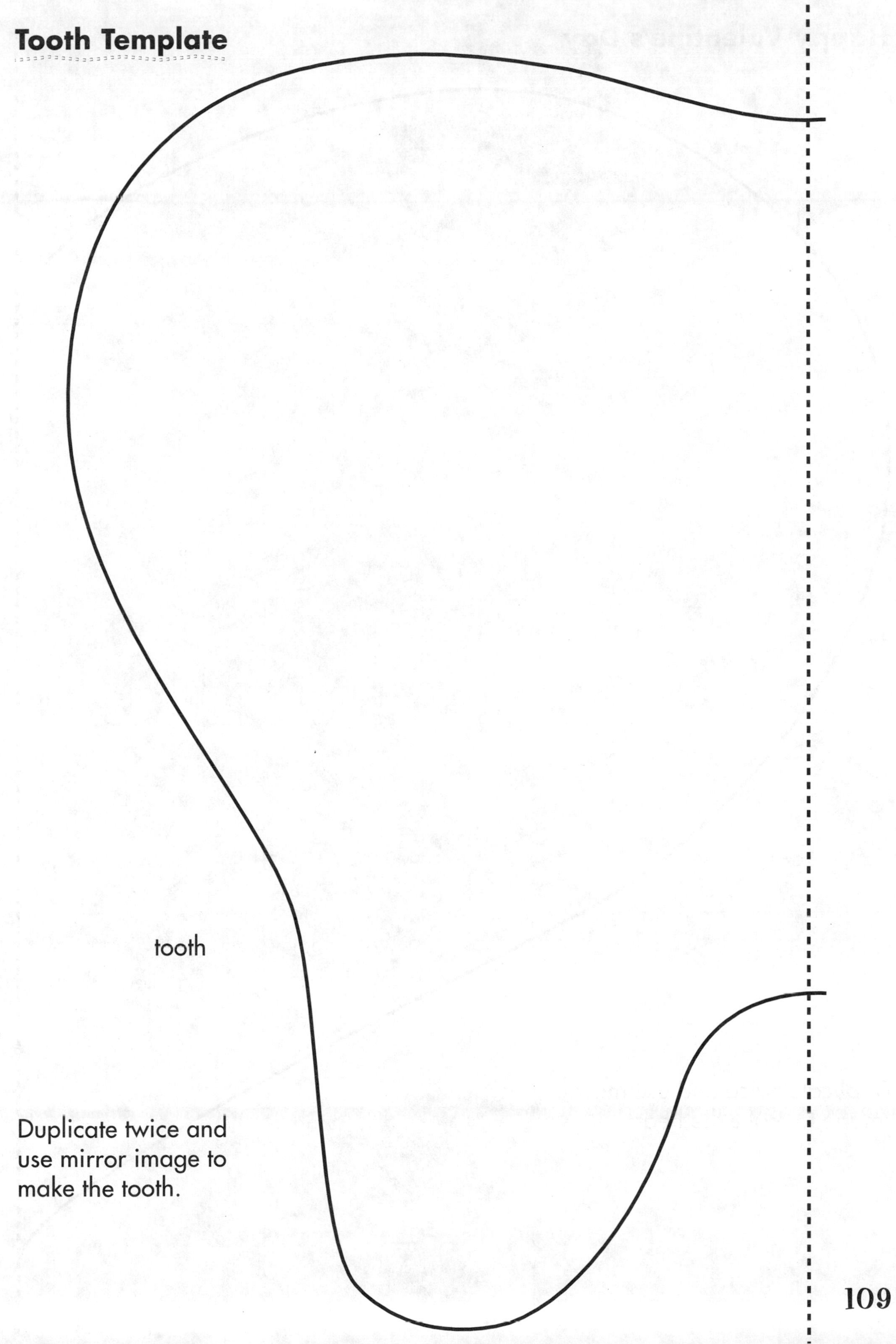

Duplicate twice and use mirror image to make the tooth.

Duplicate twice and use mirror image to make the heart.

Lunch Box

Duplicate twice and use mirror image to make the lunchbox.

lunch box

peanut butter sandwich

cookie

carrot

celery

More Uses for Pocket Charts and Sentence Strips

There are many others uses for sentence strips and pocket charts. Any time you want to write something neatly for display, think of a sentence strip. If you're looking for a place to keep small items to display things for children to see and touch, a pocket chart just might do the trick.

Bulletin Boards

Sentence strips can be used on bulletin boards. You can:

- Tell a story by writing one sentence on each strip. Display with artwork that illustrates the story. When you take the bulletin board down, glue art and sentence strip to paper and bind into a book.
- Write a poem on sentence strips. Display the poem to set the theme of the bulletin board. Decorate around the sentence strips.
- Attach sentence strips to the tops or bottoms of a 12" x 18" piece of paper and display. When you take the bulletin board down, bind the pages into a book.
- Reinforce math skills by writing equations on sentence strips and displaying when working with manipulative materials.
- Label a mural.
- Make your own alphabet frieze by writing words on sentence strips and displaying.

On Tables

Sentence strips can be placed on tables around the room:

- Place sentence strips in centers for word match or match practice.
- Write numbers 1–10 on sentence strips for children to copy correctly.
- Write children's names on sentence strips for handwriting practice.

Pocket charts make great displays. Charts can be used to hold:

- class photos
- postcards
- special awards
- small books